DATE DUE

Simulation of

COMPUTER COMMUNICATION SYSTEMS

To Caroline and Elizabeth Sauer, Elizabeth, John and Scott MacNair

Simulation of

COMPUTER COMMUNICATION SYSTEMS

Charles H. Sauer

IBM Communications Products Division
Austin, Texas 78758

Edward A. MacNair

IBM Thomas J. Watson Research Center
Yorktown Heights, New York 10598

PRENTICE-HALL, INC., Englewood Cliffs, New Jersey 07632

Library of Congress Cataloging in Publication Data

Sauer, Charles H.
   Simulation of computer communication systems.

   Bibliography: p.
   Includes index.
   1. Computer networks—Simulation methods.
2. Queuing theory.   I. MacNair, Edward A.   II. Title.
TK5105.5.S27   1983   001.64'404   83-8711
ISBN   0-13-811125-1

© 1983 by PRENTICE-HALL, INC.,
Englewood Cliffs, New Jersey   07632

Printed in the United States of America

10   9   8   7   6   5   4   3   2   1

ISBN   0-13-811125-1

PRENTICE-HALL INTERNATIONAL, INC., *London*
PRENTICE-HALL OF AUSTRALIA PTY. LIMITED, *Sydney*
EDITORA PRENTICE-HALL DO BRASIL, LTDA., *Rio de Janeiro*
PRENTICE-HALL OF CANADA, INC., *Toronto*
PRENTICE-HALL OF INDIA PRIVATE LIMITED, *New Delhi*
PRENTICE-HALL OF JAPAN, INC., *Tokyo*
PRENTICE-HALL OF SOUTHEAST ASIA PTE. LTD., *Singapore*
WHITEHALL BOOKS LIMITED, *Wellington, New Zealand*

CONTENTS

PREFACE   xi

1

INTRODUCTION   1

    1.1. Computer Communication Systems. 1
    1.2. Performance Evaluation Methodology. 2
    1.3. Further Reading. 8

2

QUEUEING MODELS   9

    2.1. Single Queue Models. 9
        2.1.1 The M/M/1 Queue. 10
        2.1.2 The M/G/1 Queue. 12
        2.1.3 The M/G/1 Queue with Message Classes. 14
    2.2. Queueing Networks. 17
        2.2.1 Open Networks. 18
        2.2.2 Closed Networks. 22
            2.2.2.1 Closed Network Characteristics. 22
            2.2.2.2 Closed Network Solutions. 27
        2.2.3 General Product Form Networks. 31
    2.3. Further Reading. 32

3

EXTENDED QUEUEING NETWORKS   **33**

    3.1. Basic Queueing Networks. 34

        3.1.1 Active Queues. 34

        3.1.2 Sources and Sink. 35

        3.1.3 Routing and Routing Chains. 36

    3.2. Network Variables and Functions. 37

        3.2.1 Variable Declaration, Naming and Assignment. 38

        3.2.2 Job Variables. 39

        3.2.3 Chain Variables. 40

        3.2.4 Global Variables. 42

        3.2.5 Distribution Functions. 43

        3.2.6 Routing Predicates. 47

        3.2.7 Status Functions. 47

    3.3. Passive Queues. 48

    3.4. Split, Fission and Fusion Nodes. 50

4

THE RESEARCH QUEUEING PACKAGE (RESQ)   **54**

    4.1. Simulation Specific Issues. 55

        4.1.1 Confidence Intervals. 55

        4.1.2 Stopping Rules. 58

    4.2. Network Definition. 58

    4.3. Submodel Definition. 69

    4.4. Further Reading. 73

5

PROTOCOL REPRESENTATIONS   75

5.1. Modular Representations. 75

5.2. Acknowledgements. 81

5.3. Time Outs. 84

Exercise 5.1 - Negative Acknowledgements without Time Outs. 91

Exercise 5.2 - Negative Acknowledgements and Time Outs. 91

Exercise 5.3 - Store and Forward Buffering. 91

Exercise 5.4 - Congestion Control. 92

5.4. Packetized Messages. 92

Exercise 5.5 - Packetized Messages and Time Outs. 96

5.5. Adaptive Routing. 96

Exercise 5.6 - Quadratic Adaptive Routing. 101

Exercise 5.7 - Routing Estimate Updating. 101

5.6. Flow Control. 102

6

LOCAL AREA NETWORKS   108

6.1. Polling Protocols. 108

Exercise 6.1 - Polling representation. 114

6.2. CSMA/CD Protocols. 114

6.3. Token Protocols. 122

7

COMPUTER SYSTEM EXAMPLES   131

7.1. Multitasking. 131

7.2. Spooling. 136

7.3. Channel-Device Interaction. 141

8

CONCLUSION   148

BIBLIOGRAPHY   **151**

INDEX   **154**

LIST OF FIGURES

Figure 1.1 - Long Haul Communication Network 1

Figure 1.2 - Queueing Network Model 3

Figure 1.3 - Extended Queueing Network Model 5

Figure 2.1 - Queue in Isolation 10

Figure 2.2 - Mean Queueing Time for M/M/1 Queue 11

Figure 2.3 - Mean Queueing Time for M/G/1 Queue 13

Figure 2.4 - Queue with Two Sources and Two Message Classes 14

Figure 2.5 - Mean Queueing Time for M/G/1 with Message Classes . . 14

Figure 2.6 - Open Queueing Network 19

Figure 2.7 - Mean Response Time in Open Product Form Network 20

Figure 2.8 - Central Server Model 22

Figure 2.9 - Central Server Model with Terminals 23

Figure 2.10 - Multiple Class Model with Terminals 24

Figure 2.11 - Two Chain Model with Terminals 25

Figure 2.12 - Closed Network Model of Window Flow Control 25

Figure 2.13 - Mean Response Time and Throughput 29

Figure 2.14 - Mixed Open and Closed Routing Chains 31

Figure 3.1 - Active Queues 35

Figure 3.2 - Source and Sink 36

Figure 3.3 - Set Node 38

Figure 3.4 - Series Queues with Interdependence 39

Figure 3.5 - Time Dependent Arrival Rates 41

Figure 3.6 - BE (Branching Erlang) Distribution 44

Figure 3.7 - Passive Queue 48

Figure 3.8 - Split, Fission and Fusion Nodes 50

Figure 3.9 - Nesting of Fission and Fusion Nodes 52

Figure 4.1 - Network without Independence Assumption 59

Figure 4.2 - Computer System Model with Memory 70

Figure 4.3 - Computer System Submodel 70

Figure 4.4 - Network with Submodel Invocation 70

Figure 5.1 - Cities Represented by Submodels 75

Figure 5.2 - City Submodel 75

Figure 5.3 - City Submodel with Acknowledgements 81

Figure 5.4 - City Submodel with Time Outs 84

Figure 5.5 - City Submodel with Packetized Messages 92

Figure 5.6 - City Submodel with Delay Statistics   96
Figure 5.7 - City Submodel with Flow Control   102
Figure 6.1 - Polling of Terminals   108
Figure 6.2 - CSMA/CD Representation   115
Figure 6.3 - Token Ring Bridge Representation   122
Figure 6.4 - Token Ring Terminal Representation   122
Figure 7.1 - CPU-I/O Multitasking   131
Figure 7.2 - Printer Spooling   136
Figure 7.3 - Channel-Device Interaction   141

PREFACE

Computer communication networks have developed from the experimental systems of a decade ago to become a central issue in computing at all levels, from personal workstations to large mainframes. Local networks connect terminals, small computers and peripheral devices in schools, stores, offices, factories, financial institutions, etc. Networks on a larger geographic scale allow sharing of computational facilities, software and data among distant individuals and enterprises. There is every reason to believe that the current proliferation of computer communication systems will at least continue until buildings without computers and involvement in computer communication systems will be unusual.

Enormous resources and expense go into this global collection of communicating computers. In spite of progress in communication technology, data communication over significant distances is expensive, often the most expensive aspect of computer communication systems. Computer hardware continues to show dramatic improvement in cost/performance ratios, but users seem to manage to quickly find use for any new computer capacity they can afford. Thus performance has remained and is likely to remain a significant issue in computing systems and computer communication systems. For the foreseeable future there will be a need to design systems for the best performance practically attainable within budget constraints.

In the design and development of systems, measurement is not feasible. *Modeling* is necessary in system design and development to estimate the performance that will be attained once a system is implemented. Traditionally there have been two approaches to modeling computer communication systems, "analytic modeling" and (discrete event) simulation. Analytic modeling is based on sufficient abstraction of systems that probability theory and other tools of applied mathematics can be used to develop equations characterizing system performance. Once the equations are developed, numerical methods are usually used to solve the equations for the desired performance measures. Analytic models have been very attractive because of the relatively small computational requirements of the numerical solutions, as compared with simulation, because the modeling problems have been intellectually stimulating and because of problems with simulation other than computational expense. However, analytic models often require such a high degree of abstraction, in order for the formulation and solution of the equations to be tractable, that in many situations it is questionable whether the models have sufficient accuracy for making choices between competing design alternatives.

As computational hardware has become dramatically less expensive, the computational requirements of simulation have become much less of a problem. Simulation has the advantage over the required abstractions of analytic models that essentially arbitrary detail may be added to a simulation model. Thus, when properly used, simulation is appropriate to decision making in system design and development situations where analytic models are of little help. Simulation is not without potential problems. Besides being its greatest advantage, the generality of simulation is a potentially severe liability, for simulation models may become intractably unwieldy because of excess detail. The running of a simulation should be viewed as an experiment which entails statistical problems as in other empirical studies. Fortunately, relatively recent work in the statistical analysis of discrete event simulations has provided methods for satisfactorily dealing with the statistical variability of simulation.

Given that the potential problems of computational expense, excess detail and statistical variability in simulation can be satisfactorily handled, there is still the effort required to construct simulation models. In the past constructing a simulation model has usually meant writing a program in a (language similar to a) programming language. In recent years a number of pieces of software have been developed which provide a higher level framework for constructing simulation models of computer communication systems (and other systems with similar characteristics). The framework is based on the *queueing network,* the usual framework used in analytic models of computer communication systems. Extensions to the queueing network make it a very flexible and expressive representation of computer communication systems. The Research Queueing Package (RESQ) is widely regarded as the best example of such software for simulation of extended queueing networks. Using a tool such as RESQ, construction of simulation models becomes a relatively effortless process.

The purpose of this book is to present modern simulation methodology as it applies to the simulation of computer communication systems. The focus is on representation of these systems by extended queueing networks. We also discuss the statistical issues and other considerations that arise in developing such simulation models. The actual models we show are constructed and simulated using RESQ. Our emphasis in these examples is on models and simulation methodology; these examples could be constructed and simulated using other software packages. (The examples could also be constructed and simulated using the Pascal extended queueing network simulation programs in Chapter 7 of Sauer and Chandy [19] and refinements of those programs.)

Chapter 1 gives a more thorough introduction to the topics covered here and more of an overview of the remainder of the book. Chapter 2 discusses the queueing models that are used in analytic models of computer communication systems. Chapter 3 summarizes the extensions to queueing networks that have recently made simulation a more attractive approach to system modeling. Chapter 4 introduces the characteristics of RESQ, including its capabilities for macro definition of submodels and its several components for statistical analysis of simulation runs. The remaining chapters develop specific aspects of simulating computer communication systems. A major issue in communication systems are the protocols used between communicating elements. Chapter 5 considers representation of basic protocols of communication networks, such as acknowledgement, packetizing of messages and flow control. Chapter 6 shows how the elements of extended queueing networks can be naturally used to represent protocols for multidrop lines and local area networks. Many of the analytic models of computer communication systems focus almost entirely on the communication aspects and make very simplistic assumptions about the computing systems involved. Chapter 7 shows how the elements of extended queueing networks facilitate appropriate representations of computing systems.

This book is intended to be useful to anyone involved in design and development of computer communication systems. As such it may be used directly by practitioners as well as in courses on computer communications systems, systems modeling, operating systems and related topics. The book is basically self contained, though it does presume some familiarity with computer communication systems and some exposure to basic concepts of probability theory.

ACKNOWLEDGEMENTS

We are grateful for the support of the Computer Science Department of the IBM Thomas J. Watson Research Center in both the development of the concepts presented in this book and the preparation of the book itself. We would like to thank K.V. Karlstrom for his suggestion of general strategy in presentation of these concepts and for his continuing editorial support.

We also thank Academic Press, Inc. for granting permission to include material originally published in the following:

S. S. Lavenberg and C. H. Sauer, "Analytical Results for Queueing Models," Chapter 3 of S. S. Lavenberg, editor, *Computer Performance Modeling Handbook,* Academic Press, Inc., New York (1983).

S. S. Lavenberg and C. H. Sauer, "Approximate Analysis Techniques for Queueing Networks," Chapter 4 of S. S. Lavenberg, editor, *Computer Performance Modeling Handbook,* Academic Press, Inc., New York (1983).

C. H. Sauer and E.A. MacNair, "Extended Queueing Network Models," Chapter 8 of S. S. Lavenberg, editor, *Computer Performance Modeling Handbook,* Academic Press, Inc., New York (1983).

The development of the extended queueing networks and of RESQ has been an evolutionary process with substantial contributions by many persons. Discussions with K.M. Chandy, D.V. Foster and C.N. Waggoner provided the original concept of simulation based on extensions to analytically tractable queueing networks. M. Reiser and L.S. Woo made substantial contributions to the initial version of RESQ and the definition of extended queueing networks used by that version. J.F. Kurose and S. Salza helped define the syntax and semantics of the language used in the current version of RESQ and implemented the translator for that language. A. Blum, P. Heidelberger, E. Jaffe, P. Rosenfeld, S. Tucci and P.D. Welch all contributed to the definition and implementation of the numerical and simulation components of RESQ. Discussions with K. Bharath-Kumar and P. Kermani have helped demonstrate the application of extended queueing networks through their extensive application of RESQ in modeling systems developed using the IBM Systems Network Architecture. Finally, we are indebted to numerous RESQ users for the many suggestions we have received, for the discussions that have helped focus our thinking and improve RESQ, and for the encouragement we have received in the development of this methodology and this tool.

Charles H. Sauer
Edward A. MacNair
March 3, 1983

Simulation of

COMPUTER COMMUNICATION SYSTEMS

CHAPTER 1

INTRODUCTION

1.1. COMPUTER COMMUNICATION SYSTEMS

Computer communication networks have developed from the experimental systems of a decade ago to become a central issue in computing at all levels, from personal workstations to large mainframes. A decade ago ARPANET was one of the few examples of an operational computer network covering a significant geographic area. Today, though ARPANET still exists, it is one of many networks, most of which are serious commercial ventures or ancillary to commercial ventures.

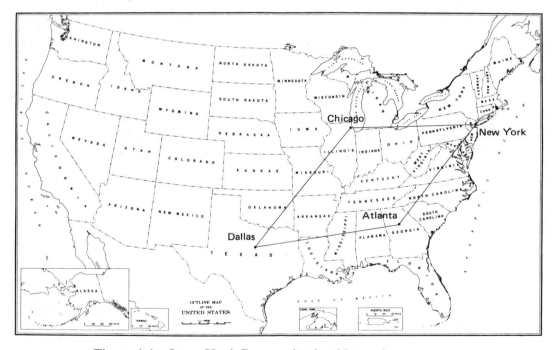

Figure 1.1 - Long Haul Communication Network

In addition to "long haul" networks such as ARPANET, local area networks have become attractive for the connection of terminals and other

1

small workstations to each other and to file servers, output devices, etc. Local (or not so local) networks connecting terminals to a common controller or computer have long been in use. However, the technology used (e.g., polled multi-drop lines) typically resulted in low bandwidths and vulnerability to component failures. Distributed control protocols, along with the technical feasibility of inexpensive stations supporting such protocols, has spurred the interest in local area networks.

Many computer communication systems will consist of both long haul and local networks, e.g., local networks connected to each other via a long haul network. There may be intermediary networks as well which are not easily classified as "local" or "long haul." Each location in the computer communication system will have some communication capability and may also have computational and file capabilities ranging from minimal to quite substantial.

In spite of progress in communication technology, data communication over significant distances is expensive, often the most expensive aspect of computer communication systems. Thus it behooves us to methodically evaluate the performance of our computer communications systems. Such evaluation can be used to either reduce cost, e.g., by using less expensive communication links where excess capacity is present, or to improve performance, e.g., by better tuning of protocols (or installation of new protocols), or both.

1.2. PERFORMANCE EVALUATION METHODOLOGY

The obvious approach to system performance evaluation is measurement of system performance. However, measurement is only feasible with operational systems. In the design and development of systems, measurement is not feasible. Further, measurement can be an unwieldy approach even in systems confined to a small geographical area because of the difficulties in obtaining the required data without affecting the measured system, because of the difficulties in obtaining reproducible measurements which are representative of the situations of interest and because of the difficulties in restructuring the system to obtain measurements for the situations of interest. Problems with measurement are exacerbated when one deals with a system with geographically dispersed components, e.g., a computer communication system.

Modeling is necessary in system design and development to estimate the performance that will be attained once a system is implemented. Modeling may be a more practical approach to performance evaluation of a working system, especially in evaluation of proposed system modifications. Modeling avoids the problems described above, i.e., it has no effect on the measured system, gives reproducible results and is amenable to evaluating alternate system structures. However, modeling has problems of its own, primarily problems of model abstraction resulting in inaccurate representation of system performance, problems of obtaining appropriate characterizations of system workload and problems of obtaining performance measures for the model.

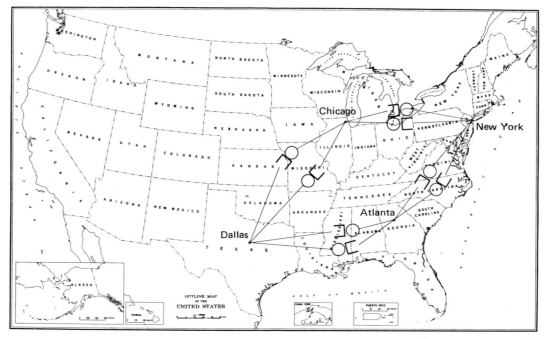

Figure 1.2 - Queueing Network Model

Performance models of computer communication systems usually focus on sharing of resources and the resulting *queueing* for resources. This is because it is usually relatively easy to quantify performance of systems

without resource sharing and the resulting contention, e.g., to predict
transmission times for messages across a communication link of given
capacity and length. (In this example, it is relatively difficult to predict the
time a message will spend waiting for its turn for transmission.)

There are two general approaches to solution of models of computer
communication systems, "analytic modeling" and "simulation." Both of
these approaches involve somewhat abstract representations of the actual
system, but typically analytic models involve much more abstraction than
simulation models. When an analytic model is appropriate, it is preferable
to simulation because of the direct relationship between the model parameters and the performance measures.

Analytic modeling is based on sufficient abstraction of systems that
probability theory and other tools of applied mathematics can be used to
develop equations characterizing system performance. Once the equations
are developed, numerical methods are usually used to solve the equations
for the desired performance measures. For an analytic model to be mathematically tractable, usually it will either represent only a single system
resource in substantial detail or it will consist of a network of queues, each
representing a resource, where the representations of the resources and their
interactions take fairly simple forms. For example, a single queue model
might represent one direction of a full duplex communication link, e.g., one
of the queues depicted in Figure 1.2. Because other components of the
system are ignored or represented in an extremely simplistic manner, details
of the single queue model such as buffer limits or priority scheduling may be
mathematically tractable. A queueing network model might represent all of
the queues depicted in Figure 1.2. In this case, the solution of the model
will usually have a *product form,* i.e., the solution consists of a product of
terms, one per resource, where the product terms may be determined essentially independently of each other. Without the existence of a product form
solution, exact analysis of a queueing network model will usually be impractical. The product form solution does not allow priority scheduling or the
simultaneous resource possession implied by consideration of buffer contention, so one would have to ignore these characteristics in the network model
of Figure 1.2. Simultaneous resource possession occurs when two or more
resources are needed at the same time.

The alternative to analytic solution of a model, discrete event simulation, is to use a program which behaves like the model and observe the behavior of the program. The principal advantage of simulation is its great generality. There are three main problems with simulation: the expense of constructing a simulation program, the computational expense of running the program, and the statistical analysis of the program behavior. In addition, since there is no direct relationship between the model parameters and the simulation results, additional runs must be made for different model parameters.

Analytic models are very attractive because of the relatively small computational requirements of the numerical solutions, as compared with simulation, because the modeling problems have been intellectually stimulating and because of the other problems with simulation just mentioned. However, analytic models often require such a high degree of abstraction, in order for the formulation and solution of the equations to be tractable, that in many situations it is questionable whether the models have sufficient accuracy for making choices between competing design alternatives.

As computational hardware has become dramatically less expensive, the computational requirements of simulation have become much less of a problem. Simulation has the advantage over the required abstractions of analytic models that essentially arbitrary detail may be added to a simulation model. Thus, when properly used, simulation is appropriate to decision making in system design and development situations where analytic models are of little help. Besides being its greatest advantage, the generality of simulation is a potentially severe liability, for simulation models may become intractably unwieldy because of excess detail. The running of a simulation should be viewed as an experiment which entails statistical problems as in other empirical studies. Fortunately, relatively recent work in the statistical analysis of discrete event simulations has provided methods for satisfactorily dealing with the statistical variability of simulation.

Given that the potential problems of computational expense, excess detail and statistical variability in simulation can be satisfactorily handled, there is still the effort required to construct simulation models. In the past, constructing a simulation model has usually meant writing a program in a (language similar to a) programming language. In recent years a number of

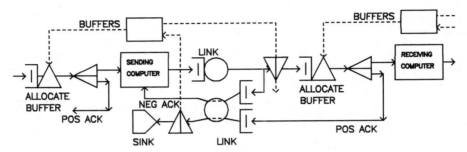

Figure 1.3 - Extended Queueing Network Model

pieces of software have been developed which provide a higher level framework for constructing simulation models of computer communication systems (and other systems with similar characteristics). The framework is
based on the queueing networks usually used in analytic models of computer
communication systems. Extensions to the queueing network make it a very
flexible and expressive representation of computer communication systems.
Figure 1.3 illustrates an extended queueing network model of part of a
computer communication system, with a "passive queue" used to represent
buffer contention and a "split node" used to generate acknowledgement
messages.

In order to effectively use queueing networks as performance models,
appropriate software is necessary for definition of the networks to be
solved, for solution of the networks (by numerical, approximate and/or
simulation methods) and for examination of the performance measures
obtained. The Research Queueing Package (RESQ) which we have constructed is an example of such software for simulation of extended queueing
networks. Using a tool such as RESQ, construction of simulation models
becomes a relatively effortless process.

Tools similar to RESQ include the Queueing Network Analysis Package
(QNAP) [13] and the Performance Analyst's Workbench System (PAWS)
[4]. Construction of the simulation components of such tools is discussed in

Chapter 7 of Sauer and Chandy [19]. That chapter includes Pascal programs for an extended queueing network simulation system and exercises suggesting further development of those programs. Those programs as given are sufficient for simulating some of the networks we use as examples. By performing the appropriate exercises, the reader would have a simulation system capable of simulating all of our examples. (However, the system as given does not have the user interface capabilities of RESQ, i.e., the networks to be simulated are defined by writing a Pascal program which calls the simulation system.)

The purpose of this book is to present modern simulation methodology as it applies to the simulation of computer communication systems. The focus is on representation of these systems by extended queueing networks. We also discuss the statistical issues and other considerations that arise in developing such simulation models. The actual models we show are constructed and simulated using RESQ. Our emphasis in these examples is on models and simulation methodology; these examples could be constructed and simulated using other software packages.

Chapter 2 discusses the queueing models that are used in analytic models of computer communication systems. Chapter 3 summarizes the extensions to queueing networks that have recently made simulation a more attractive approach to system modeling. Chapter 4 introduces the characteristics of RESQ, including its capabilities for macro definition of submodels and its several components for statistical analysis of simulation runs.

The remaining chapters develop specific aspects of simulating computer communication systems. We have chosen not to organize these chapters around any particular model of communication system design, e.g., the International Organization for Standardization's Reference Model of Open Systems Interconnection (ISO OSI) or IBM's Systems Network Architecture (SNA). Reasons for this choice include the fact that these and other models of communication system architecture are still competing for acceptance, that these architectural models are oriented toward function and specific implementation issues while our performance models are oriented toward abstraction and that issues present in several layers of ISO OSI or SNA can be considered collectively from a performance modeling viewpoint. For example, window flow control mechanisms are present in several layers of ISO OSI and SNA but can be represented in essentially the same manner in our extended queueing network models.

Chapter 5 considers representation of basic protocols of communication networks, such as acknowledgement, packetizing of messages and flow control. Chapter 6 shows how the elements of extended queueing networks can be naturally used to represent protocols for local networks and multi-drop lines. Many of the analytic models of computer communication systems focus almost entirely on the communication aspects and make very simplistic assumptions about the computing systems involved. Chapter 7 shows how the elements of extended queueing networks facilitate appropriate representations of computing systems.

1.3. FURTHER READING

An excellent introduction to computer communication systems is given by Tanenbaum [31]. See also Tanenbaum's survey article on protocols [32]. Sauer and Chandy [19] introduce many of the concepts of performance modeling relevant to the issues considered here. See also Kleinrock Volume II [9] and Schwartz [29].

CHAPTER 2

QUEUEING MODELS

Mathematically solved models of performance of computer communication systems are usually focused on queueing for system resources. Queueing models have been used to evaluate the performance of communication systems since Erlang's work with telephone systems at the turn of the century. The solution and application of queueing models has been a significant area of applied mathematics and probability theory for decades. Queueing models have been used in computer communication applications since the mid-sixties [7].

For the solution of a queueing model to be mathematically tractable, assumptions must be made about the modeled system. Typically these assumptions relate to the process(es) of arrivals at the queue(s), the service process(es) at the queues and the scheduling discipline(s) used at the queue(s). When the model consists of a single queue representing a single resource (or a collection of homogeneous resources) then the assumptions need not be as restrictive for sake of tractability as when the model consists of several queues representing several distinct resources.

We will first briefly survey results for single queue models and then results for queueing network models. This is done to give the reader a feel for what is practical in terms of mathematically tractable models of computer communication systems. Mathematically tractable models are useful in their own right, but our motive is more to provide a basis for discussing the extended queueing networks we advocate for simulation of computer communication systems. We will not present derivations of equations since that would detract from our primary intent. Derivations may be found in the references cited in Section 2.3 and listed in the Bibliography.

2.1. SINGLE QUEUE MODELS

Models consisting of a single queue are usually used for evaluation of communication links, though such models are also used for evaluation of

9

processors, direct access storage devices and other resources. The simplest model in such applications is the classical "M/M/1" queue. The three positions in this classical notation characterize the arrival process, the service process and the number of servers, respectively. (Other information, e.g., the scheduling discipline, is left implicit or separately stated. When left implicit, the scheduling discipline is assumed to be First Come First Served (FCFS). Another implicit assumption is that the queue is allowed to become arbitrarily large.) The "M" stands for "Markov" indicating exponential interarrival times (a Poisson arrival process) and exponential service times. It is assumed that there is a source of items, which we will usually refer to as "messages" or "jobs," and that this source is inexhaustible. (Usually we will refer to these items as "messages" when discussing models of communication and as "jobs" when discussing models of computer systems. However, we will sometimes refer to "jobs" even when discussing models of communication systems.) Items arriving from the source go to the queue and jobs leaving the queue go to a sink, as depicted in Figure 2.1.

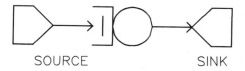

SOURCE   SINK

Figure 2.1 - Queue in Isolation

2.1.1. The M/M/1 Queue

Let us assume the arrival process has rate λ jobs per time unit (i.e., mean interarrival time $1/\lambda$). Let us assume the service process has mean service time S (i.e., mean service rate $1/S$). The queue will be stable if the server is not saturated, i.e., as long as the service rate is less than the arrival rate. The "traffic intensity," ρ, is defined as the ratio of the arrival rate and the service rate, i.e., $\rho = \lambda S$. Thus the queue is stable provided that $\rho < 1$. The utilization of the server will be equal to the traffic intensity, provided the server is not saturated. Let us call the throughput R. Assuming the queue is stable, $R = \lambda$.

In using the M/M/1 queue as a model of a simple communication link, λ will be the rate of arrival of messages (or packets) at the link, and S will be the mean time for transmission of messages (or packets). The assumption of exponential interarrival times may or may not be reasonable, depending on the modeled system. The transmission time for a message will be the propagation delay plus the message length divided by the link capacity. If the propagation delay is negligible compared to the length divided by the link capacity, then the reasonableness of the exponential service time assumption depends primarily on whether the message lengths are reasonably represented by an exponential distribution. For example, consider a link from New York to Atlanta, a distance of approximately 1225 kilometers. The propagation delay will be approximately $1225/3 \times 10^5$ seconds or 4.08 milliseconds. For an 80 bit message on a 9600 baud link, the propagation delay would be roughly a third of the total transmission time of 12.41 ms. For a 2000 bit message on a 2400 baud link, the propagation delay would less than 0.5% of the total transmission time of 837.4 ms.

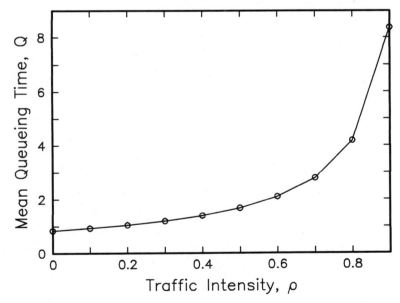

Figure 2.2 - Mean Queueing Time for M/M/1 Queue

For the M/M/1 queue, the mean queue length, including messages in transmission, is

$$L = \frac{\rho^2}{1-\rho} + \rho = \frac{\rho}{1-\rho}$$

For example, if $\lambda = 1/2$ message per second and $S = 0.8374$ seconds, then $\rho = 0.4187$ and $L = 0.7203$ messages. The mean queueing (response) time, including transmission time, is

$$Q = \frac{S\rho}{1-\rho} + S = \frac{S}{(1-\rho)}$$

For example, if $S = 0.8374$ seconds and $\rho = 0.4187$, then $Q = 1.441$ seconds. The queueing time distribution is exponential with mean Q. Figure 2.2 shows a plot of Q versus ρ for $S = 0.8374$ seconds. Note the sharp rise as ρ goes above roughly 0.6.

2.1.2. The M/G/1 Queue

In classical queueing notation, "G" stands for "general," i.e., the M/G/1 queue is a single server queue with exponential (Markovian) inter-arrival times and general (arbitrarily distributed) service times. We use the same notation as before, except we now also use σ for the standard deviation of service times. The M/G/1 queue is useful where the assumption of exponential service times is not satisfactory. For example, consider the 9600 baud link from New York to Atlanta. The propagation delay is fixed, i.e., it has standard deviation 0. Let us assume that the message length has an approximately exponential distribution, so the standard deviation of the transmission time related to link capacity is also $80/9600$ seconds = 8.333 ms. Since the two components of the transmission time are independent, the standard deviation of the total transmission time is the square root of the sum of squares of the component standard deviations, i.e., $\sigma = (0^2 + 8.333^2)^{0.5} = 8.333$ ms. This is considerably less than the mean total transmission time, 12.41 ms. For the exponential distribution, $\sigma = S$. Therefore, the exponential distribution does not seem to be a good fit.

For the M/G/1 queue the mean queue length is given by

$$L = \frac{\rho^2(1 + (\sigma/S)^2)}{2(1-\rho)} + \rho$$

and the mean queueing time for the M/G/1 queue is given by

$$Q = \frac{\rho S(1 + (\sigma/S)^2)}{2(1-\rho)} + S$$

Note that these equations simplify to the M/M/1 equations for $\sigma = S$. The queueing time distribution for the M/G/1 queue does not have a simple form.

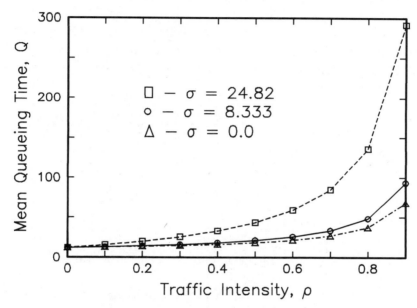

Figure 2.3 - Mean Queueing Time for M/G/1 Queue

For example, with the numbers just given ($S = 12.41$ ms. and $\sigma = 8.333$ ms.) and $\lambda = 50$ messages per second, $\rho = 0.6205$ and $L = 1.356$ and $Q = 27.12$ ms.. If we were to assume exponential service times, i.e., $\sigma = 12.41$, then we would have $L = 1.635$ and we would have $Q = 32.70$ ms. If the message length distribution were less variable than the exponential distribution, then there would be larger differences between the exponential service assumption of the M/M/1 model and the more precise characterization of the M/G/1 model. For example, if the message length was uniformly distributed over the interval [24,136], the mean length would still be 80 bits, but the standard deviation of the length would be only 32.33 as compared with 80 for the assumption of the exponential distribution. Then with a 9600 baud link the standard deviation of the time related to link capacity is 32.33/9600 seconds = 3.368 ms. and the standard deviation of the total transmission time would also be σ = 3.368 ms. With this σ and the previous values (λ = 50 messages per second, S = 12.41 ms. and ρ = 0.6205), L = 1.165 and Q = 23.30 ms. Figure 2.3 shows a plot of Q versus ρ for several values of σ, with S = 12.41 ms.

2.1.3. *The M/G/1 Queue with Message Classes*

The discussion so far has assumed that we do not wish to distinguish between different classes of messages, for example, between messages with different (origin,destination) pairs and/or between data and control messages (e.g., acknowledgements).

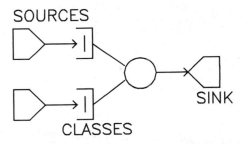

Figure 2.4 - Queue with Two Sources and Two Message Classes

2.1.3.1 FCFS Scheduling. With FCFS scheduling the extension of the M/G/1 equations (including the M/M/1 equations) is straightforward once we define notation. Let there be A sources of messages. The arrival rate of messages from source a, $a=1,...,A$, is λ_a. Let there be C message classes at the queue. Arriving messages from source a, $a=1,...,A$, belong to class c, $c=1,...,C$, with probability q_{ac}. Let the mean service time for class c messages be S_c and let the standard deviation of the service time for class c messages be σ_c. Scheduling is first come first served without regard to message class.

Let the throughput of class c messages be R_c. Assuming the queue is stable,

$$R_c = \sum_{a=1}^{A} \lambda_a q_{ac}$$

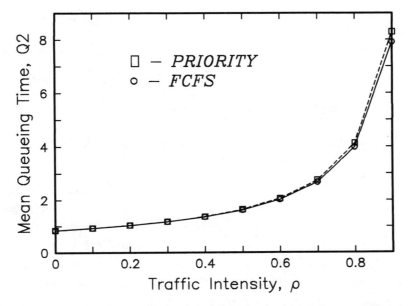

Figure 2.5 - Mean Queueing Time for M/G/1 with Message Classes

The overall arrival rate of messages is

$$\lambda = \sum_{c=1}^{C} R_c$$

Again assuming stability, the overall mean service time will be

$$S = \frac{\sum\limits_{c=1}^{C} R_c S_c}{\lambda}$$

and the overall standard deviation of service time will be

$$\sigma = \sqrt{\frac{\sum\limits_{c=1}^{C} R_c(\sigma_c^2 + S_c^2)}{\lambda} - S^2}$$

With these definitions, ρ, R, L and Q are obtained as before and the queue is stable if and only if $\rho < 1$. The class specific utilization is the class specific traffic intensity

$$\rho_c = R_c S_c$$

The class specific mean queue length is given by

$$L_c = \frac{R_c}{R} \frac{\rho^2(1 + (\sigma/S)^2)}{2(1-\rho)} + \rho_c$$

and the class specific mean queueing time is given by

$$Q_c = \frac{\rho S(1 + (\sigma/S)^2)}{2(1-\rho)} + S_c$$

For example, let us return to the first set of parameters we considered for the M/M/1 queue, i.e., messages with mean length of 2000 bits with an exponential distribution, a 2400 baud link and a 4.08 ms. propagation delay, arriving at a rate of 1/2 message per second. Let us assume that these are data messages and refer to them as class 2. Let class 1 consist of control messages of constant length 20 bits, arriving at a rate of 2 messages per second. Let there be two sources corresponding to the two classes of messages. Then $\lambda_1 = 2$ messages per second and $\lambda_2 = 0.5$ message per second. $q_{11} = q_{22} = 1$, and $q_{12} = q_{21} = 0$. Thus $R_1 = 2$ messages per second and $R_2 = 0.5$ message per second. $S_1 = 12.41$ ms., $\rho_1 = 0.0248$, $S_2 = 837.4$ ms. and $\rho_2 = 0.4187$. $\lambda = 2.5$ messages per second. $S = 0.8 \times 12.41 + 0.2 \times 837.4 = 177.4$ and $\rho = .4435$. $\sigma_1 = 0$ and $\sigma_2 = 833.3$, so $\sigma = (0.2 \times (833.3^2 + 837.4^2) - 177.4^2)^{0.5} = 497.6$ ms. Finally, $L = 2.011$, $Q = 804.3$ ms., $L_1 = 1.279$, $L_2 = 0.732$, $Q_1 = 639.3$ ms. and $Q_2 = 1.464$ seconds. Thus the control messages are experiencing mean delays more than 50 times their transmission times. Figure 2.5 shows a plot of Q_2 versus ρ with $S_1 = 12.41$ ms., $S_2 = 837.4$ ms. and $\lambda_1 = 4\lambda_2$ for both FCFS and the priority scheduling we now discuss.

2.1.3.2 Priority Scheduling. In the above example we naturally wonder what improvement would be obtained by giving control messages priority over data messages. It is reasonable to expect that this will have small effect on the data messages while significantly reducing delays for control messages (and thus perhaps improving responsiveness elsewhere in the system). Let us assume that the control messages (class 1) are given non-preemptive priority over the data messages (class 2). With non-preemptive priority scheduling, lower priority messages, which have begun transmission, are permitted to finish even if higher priority messages arrive. The class 1 (higher priority) mean queueing time is given by

$$Q_1 = \frac{\rho S(1 + (\sigma/S)^2)}{2(1-\rho_1)} + S_1$$

The class 2 (lower priority) mean queueing time is given by

$$Q_2 = \frac{\rho S(1 + (\sigma/S)^2)}{2(1-\rho_1)(1-\rho)} + S_2$$

For either class, $L_c = R_c Q_c$. $L = L_1 + L_2$ and $Q = L/\lambda$.

Returning to our numerical values, with non-preemptive priority we now have $Q_1 = 370.1$ ms. and $Q_2 = 1.480$ seconds. The mean delay for control messages is dramatically reduced when they are given priority, with negligible adverse effect on the mean delay for data messages. $L_1 = .740$, $L_2 = .740$, $L = 1.480$ and $Q = 592$ ms.

2.1.3.3 Other Scheduling Disciplines and Characteristics. The M/G/1 queue is mathematically tractable with a variety of other scheduling disciplines and characteristics. The above discussion of non-preemptive priority with two message classes extends to an arbitrary number of classes and to other priority schemes such as preemptive priority. Scheduling disciplines used in polling of multidrop lines have been treated extensively. Scheduling disciplines useful in processor scheduling, particularly the "processor sharing" discipline, a limiting case of a round robin (time slicing) discipline as the quantum (time slice) tends to zero, are also tractable [9].

A variety of other characteristics in single queue models are also tractable. Some of these include multiple server queues, service rates dependent on queue length, arrival rates dependent on queue length, finite capacity for waiting messages, group arrivals, etc. We will not discuss these characteristics here since these models have been given substantial mathematical treatment elsewhere.

2.2. QUEUEING NETWORKS

Separate models, each representing a single resource, will usually be inadequate for evaluation of overall system performance because of strong interactions and dependencies between resources. Queueing network models are more appropriate for evaluation of overall system performance because they can represent these interactions and dependencies. Unfortunately, many of the things we would like to include in queueing network models, including some of the characteristics we just discussed in regard to single queue models, are not mathematically tractable. Thus simulation is often more appropriate than a mathematically tractable model.

Mathematically tractable queueing network models usually either have a *product form* solution, or are small (measured in terms of numbers of queues or maximum number of messages in the network or some similar characteristic). Most useful mathematically tractable queueing network models have the product form solution. In its simplest form, the product form solution says that the probability of a given distribution of messages among queues of the network is given by the product of probabilities of the corresponding numbers of jobs at isolated M/M/1 queues, i.e., in a network of M queues,

$$P(n_1,...,n_M) = P_1(n_1)...P_M(n_M)$$

$P(n_1,...,n_M)$ is the probability of n_1 messages at queue 1, n_2 messages at queue 2, ..., n_M messages at queue M, and $P_m(n_m)$, $m = 1,...,M$, is the probability of n_m messages at queue m in isolation, assuming that queue m is an M/M/1 queue with an appropriately chosen arrival rate.

A key assumption in using product form queueing networks of communication systems is Kleinrock's "independence assumption" [7,9] This assumption says that transmission times for a given message on different links are independent. Clearly this is not the case, assuming the message length does not change, for the transmission time is directly determined by the message length. However, Kleinrock argues that usually this assumption does not significantly affect performance results and makes mathematical analysis tractable. One will normally avoid this assumption using simulation, of course.

We first consider two important special classes of product form networks and then discuss some of the characteristics which may be allowed in general product form networks.

2.2.1. Open Networks

An open network is one with external arrivals from sources and departures through sinks, as in the single queue models we have considered already. See Jackson [6] for an early discussion of open networks. A closed network has a fixed population of messages (jobs). As in the M/G/1 queue with message classes, let us assume that there are A sources. Let us assume arrivals from source a have exponential interarrival times with rate λ_a. Let there be C message classes in the sense of Section 2.1.3. Let there be M queues. The classes are partitioned among the queues, with at least one class per queue. Let $\mathscr{C}_m$ be the set of classes belonging to queue m. Queue m has FCFS scheduling and exponential service times with mean S_m at each of its classes. The product form solution requires that FCFS queues have exponential service time distributions with each class of a queue having the same mean. General, class specific distributions are allowed by the product form solution for certain special scheduling disciplines (processor sharing, last come first serve and infinite server) [2]. Let the probability a message arriving from source a goes to class c be designated q_{ac}. Let the probability a message departing from class i goes to class j be designated p_{ij} and let the probability a message departing from class i goes to a sink be designated p_{i0}. Assuming all queues are stable, the solutions to the set of equations

$$R_c = \sum_{a=1}^{A} \lambda_a q_{ac} + \sum_{i=1}^{C} R_c p_{ic}, \ c = 1,...,C,$$

give the arrival rates at each of the classes. Let $R_{(m)} = \sum_c R_c$ be the arrival rate at queue m, where the summation is taken over the classes of queue m. Queue m then has traffic intensity $\rho_m = R_{(m)} S_m$. Its mean queue length and mean queueing time are the same as those given for the M/M/1 queue in Section 2.1.1. Since the mean service times are the same for all classes at queue m, the mean queueing times are also the same for all classes at queue m. The mean queue length for class c at queue m will be $L_m R_c / R_{(m)}$. The mean number of messages in the network is simply the sum of the mean queue lengths, and the mean response time for a message is the sum of the mean queueing times for the queues it visits.

For example, consider the queueing network of Figure 2.6, based on the networks of Figures 1.1 and 1.2. This represents sources of messages

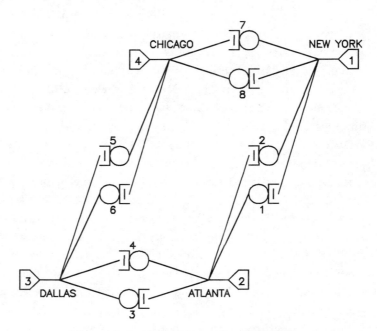

Figure 2.6 - Open Queueing Network

and sinks for messages at each of the four cities and four 9600 baud full
duplex links between pairs of cities. Each half duplex link is represented by
a queue. Let us assume that a message from one city is equally likely to go
to each of the other cities, e.g., a message from New York is equally likely
to go to Atlanta, Dallas or Chicago. A message will be routed so as to
minimize the number of hops. When two minimal hop routes are available,
each is equally likely to be chosen, e.g., a message from Atlanta to Chicago
is equally likely to go through New York or Dallas.

Given these assumptions, we can define two classes at each queue, one
for one hop messages and one for two hop messages. These classes are not
explicitly shown in the figure to avoid clutter. Let class 1 be the "one hop"
class for queue 1, class 2 be the "two hop" class for queue 1, class 3 be the
one hop class for queue 2, class 4 be the two hop class for queue 2, etc. A
message arriving from a source, say source 1 (New York), will go to each

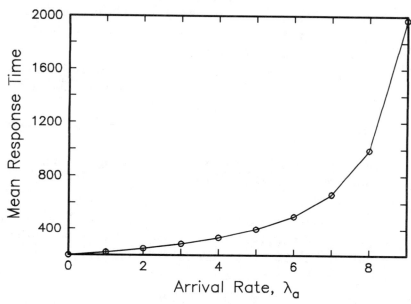

Figure 2.7 - Mean Response Time in Open Product Form Network

available one hop class (e.g., classes 1 and 15) with probability 1/3 each
and to each available two hop class (e.g., classes 2 and 16) with probability
1/6 each. A message leaving a two hop class (e.g., 2) will then go to a one
hop class (e.g., 5). If we say that each source has arrival rate $\lambda_a = 5$
messages per second, $a=1,2,3,4$, then $R_c = 5/6$ for each one hop class,
$c=1,3,...,15$, $R_c = (5/3)+(5/6)$ for each two hop class, $c=2,4,...,16$, and
$R_{(m)} = 3.333$ messages per second for $m=1,...,8$.

We determined the propagation delay between New York and Atlanta
as 4.08 ms. in Section 2.1.1. The distance from Atlanta to Dallas is approximately 1130 kilometers, so the propagation delay is approximately 3.77
ms., the distance from Dallas to Chicago is approximately 1270 km., so the
propagation delay is approximately 4.23 ms. and the distance from Chicago
to New York is also approximately 1130 km., so the propagation delay is
again approximately 3.77 ms. Let us assume that each city generates
messages of average length 1400 bits, so the mean transmission time related
to link capacity is 1400/9600 = 145.8 ms. Then for $m=1,2$ (the links
between New York and Atlanta), the mean total transmission time S_m is
149.9 ms., $\rho_m = 0.4997$, $L_m = 0.9987$ and $Q_m = 299.6$ ms. For

m=3,4,7,8, (the links between Atlanta and Dallas and between Chicago and New York) S_m is 149.6 ms., ρ_m = 0.4987, L_m = 0.9947 and Q_m = 298.4 ms. For m=5,6, (the links between Dallas and Chicago) S_m is 150.0 ms., ρ_m = 0.5000, L_m = 1.000 and Q_m = 300 ms. The mean response time for a two hop message is roughly 598 ms (300+298 ms). Since there are twice as many one hop messages as two hop messages, the mean response time for all messages is roughly 399 ms ((300+300+598)/3 ms). Figure 2.7 shows the overall mean response versus λ_a, assuming λ_a is the same for a=1,2,3,4.

There are some additional characteristics which can be added to open product form network models of communication systems. These are primarily of theoretical interest and will be briefly discussed in Section 2.2.3. Many practical characteristics (in addition to the independence assumption) are not allowed by the product form solution, including packetizing and reassembly of messages, buffering and most protocols. However, the closed product form networks we discuss in the next section have been used to represent some end to end flow control protocols.

2.2.2. Closed Networks

A closed network is one closed to arrivals from sources and departures through sinks, i.e., the number of items circulating through the network is fixed. Though closed queueing networks had been used as models of computer systems and other systems for years, it was not until Buzen proposed the "central server model" [3] that closed product form queueing networks became important as models of computer systems. Considerably more recently, closed queueing networks have been seen as useful as models of end to end flow control in communication systems.

In a closed network model, it is usually assumed that use of some resources is dependent on the possession of some other resource, and that this other resource is fully utilized. In the central server model of Figure 2.8, this other resource is memory. A job in the queueing network represents a command from a user at a terminal or an operating system task. Memory is required for using the CPU or disk devices. A job holding memory alternates back and forth between computation and input/output until the command processing is completed. The central server model

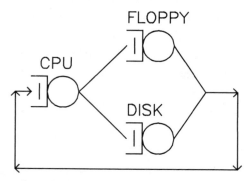

Figure 2.8 - Central Server Model

assumes that the number of jobs holding memory is fixed, and that once one job finishes, it is immediately replaced by another job.

The queues of a closed network have the same restrictions as those of an open network, e.g., that at a FCFS queue the service time distribution must be exponential, with each class having the same mean service time. In the central server model it is often assumed that the CPU queue has the Processor Sharing scheduling discipline, thus allowing a product form solution with general service time distributions at the CPU. However, with processor sharing scheduling and general service time distributions, only the mean service time affects the solution for mean values of performance measures. Assuming FCFS for the CPU, with the same mean service time but an exponential distribution results in the same product form solution and mean performance measures.

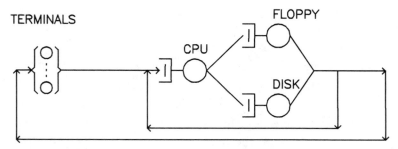

Figure 2.9 - Central Server Model with Terminals

In the central server model with terminals (Figure 2.9) the terminals
are the "other resource." A terminal is required for using the computer
system. The model assumes that the number of users at the terminals is
fixed, and that once one user finishes, he or she is immediately replaced by
another user. Note that this model ignores memory contention and that this
network has one class per queue.

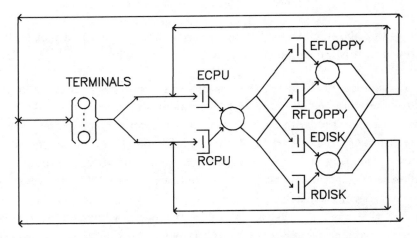

Figure 2.10 - Multiple Class Model with Terminals

The network of Figure 2.10 is a refinement of the network of Figure
2.9. Both networks may be considered models of the same computer system
and both assume that all jobs are homogeneous. The second network
distinguishes between types of commands: sometimes a user issues a command to an editor (presumably such commands are likely to have low CPU
service demands) while other times a user issues a command to run a program other than an editor (presumably these commands have higher CPU
service times). Each of the queues other than the one for the terminals has
two classes: one for editing commands and one for "running" commands.
Assuming that scheduling at the CPU is represented by the Processor
Sharing discipline, then we can have distinct service time distributions at the
two CPU classes. Assuming that device scheduling is FCFS, then the two

floppy disk classes must have the same exponential distribution and the two
hard disk classes must have the same exponential distribution, but the
floppy disk classes need not have the same mean service time as the hard
disk classes.

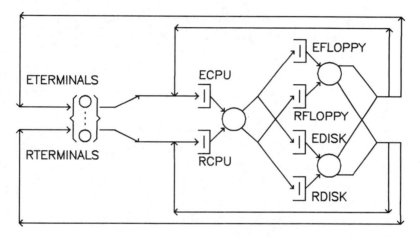

Figure 2.11 - Two Chain Model with Terminals

A major difference between closed and open networks is that in closed
networks with multiple classes it is often useful to partition the classes into
routing "chains." The network of Figure 2.11 is similar to that of Figure
2.10 but has two routing chains. The network of Figure 2.10 assumes that
homogeneous users switch (frequently) between editing and "running"
modes. In the network of Figure 2.11 there are two heterogeneous sets of
users, one set which stays in editing mode and one which stays in running
mode.

Figure 2.12 shows a closed network model of end to end flow control
corresponding to the open network model of Figure 2.6. In the open
network model, there is no limit to the number of messages which may be in
transit and queued for transmission. In a communication system with end to

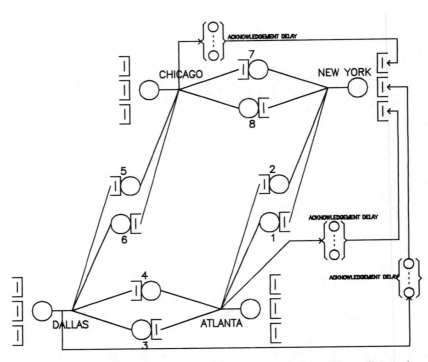

Figure 2.12 - Closed Network Model of Window Flow Control

end flow control, there is a limit (a "window") to the number of messages which may be in transit between a given source and a given destination. In the closed network model the "other" resource is (a position in) the window of the end to end protocol. A message must have a position in the window before it can be queued for transmission. There is a separate window and correspondingly separate routing chain for each (source,destination) pair. The number of customers in each routing chain is set equal to the window size, i.e., the limit to the number of messages which may be in transit between a given source and destination. Instead of the sources and sinks of the open network, there are additional queues. One single server queue effectively takes the place of the source and represents the time it takes to generate messages (i.e., by the computer system). Another queue, an "infinite server" queue (one without waiting for service), represents the time it takes acknowledgement messages to get back to the message source. This artificial queue is used rather than including the acknowledgement traffic in the queues for the links along the lines discussed in Section 2.1.3 because the product form solution does not allow the heterogeneous message classes and priority scheduling that would be necessary to properly represent the acknowledgement traffic. Figure 2.12 fully shows these queues only for the traffic originating from New York, to avoid cluttering the diagram.

For closed networks, the product form solution is not quite as simple conceptually or computationally as the product form solution for open networks. This is primarily because of the stronger interactions between the queues due to the fixed number of jobs and because the heterogeneous jobs of the different routing chains must be explicitly considered. In a network of M queues, the basic product form becomes

$$P(\vec{n}_1,...,\vec{n}_M) = \frac{X_1(\vec{n}_1)...X_M(\vec{n}_M)}{G(\vec{N})}$$

The vectors have elements corresponding to the different routing chains. $P(\vec{n}_1,...,\vec{n}_M)$ is the probability of $\vec{n}_1$ messages at queue 1, $\vec{n}_2$ messages at queue 2, ..., $\vec{n}_M$ messages at queue M, $X_m(\vec{n}_m)$, $m = 1,...,M$, is a factor determined from the probability of $\vec{n}_m$ messages at queue m in isolation, assuming that queue is an M/M/1 queue with appropriately chosen arrival rates, $\vec{N}$ is the vector of numbers of jobs in the routing chains and $G(\vec{N})$ is a normalizing constant.

In open networks, it is possible to avoid direct consideration of the product form and just consider the queues separately. In closed networks, the queues must be considered collectively, but it is not necessary for a computational algorithm to recognize the explicit product form. We now sketch the Mean Value Analysis algorithm for a closed network with a single routing chain. We use essentially the same notation as in Section 2.2.1, except that we need not consider sources and must explicitly consider the fixed number of jobs in the network.

There are C job classes and M queues. The classes are partitioned among the queues, with at least one class per queue. Let $\mathscr{C}_m$ be the set of classes belonging to queue m. Queue m has FCFS scheduling and exponential service times with mean S_m at each of its classes. Let the probability a message departing from class i goes to class j be designated p_{ij}. A solution to the set of equations

$$r_c = \sum_{i=1}^{C} r_c p_{ic}, \; c = 1,...,C,$$

gives the relative throughputs at each of the classes in the sense that if R_c is the throughput at class c, then the throughput at class d is $R_d = (r_d/r_c)R_c$. These equations are linearly dependent and thus do not have a unique set of solutions. However, any positive set of solutions is acceptable and one may be chosen arbitrarily. Let $r_{(m)} = \sum_c r_c$ be the relative throughput at queue m, where the summation is taken over the classes of queue m. Let the number of jobs in the network be N.

We will only consider single server queues and infinite server queues, since these are the most important for our models and the simplest for the algorithm. However, the algorithm applies to the full class of product form networks [18]. Let $L_m(n)$ be the mean queue length at queue m when there are n jobs in the network and $Q_m(n)$ be the mean queueing time at queue m when there are n jobs in the network.

The name of the algorithm comes from the fact that, for networks with only single server and infinite server queues, performance measures may be determined strictly from mean values, without direct consideration of probabilities of network states or marginal probabilities. For single server queues, Reiser and Lavenberg showed [14] that

$$Q_m(n) = S_m(1 + L_m(n - 1)).$$

For infinite server queues,

$$Q_m(n) = S_m.$$

Given the mean queueing time, the mean queue length is obtainable from Little's Rule and the throughput. The throughput is obtainable by applying

Little's Rule to the mean cycle time, i.e., the mean time between visits to a queue:

$$n = R_{(m)}(n) \left[\sum_{i=1}^{M} \frac{r_{(i)}}{r_{(m)}} Q_i(n) \right]$$

The population, n, of the network, is used as the "queue length" in Little's Rule. The sum on the right hand side is the mean cycle time. The equation is solved for throughput. Using these recursive equations and the initial condition that $L_m(0) = 0$, $m = 1,...,M$, we can state the following algorithm [14]:

For $n=1$ to N
    For $m=1$ to M
        If queue m is single server then
            $Q_m(n) = S_m(1 + L_m(n - 1))$
        else { queue m is single server }
            $Q_m(n) = S_m$
    End loop on m
    For $m=1$ to M

$$R_{(m)}(n) = \frac{n}{\displaystyle\sum_{i=1}^{M} \frac{r_{(i)}}{r_{(m)}} Q_i(n)}$$

        $L_m(n) = R_{(m)}(n)Q_m(n)$
    End loop on m
End loop on n

As a numerical example, consider the network of Figure 2.9. Let the mean thinking and keying time, S_1, be 10 seconds. Let the mean CPU time, S_2 be 50 ms., the mean floppy disk time, S_3 be 220 ms. and the mean hard disk time, S_4 be 19 ms. Let the probability a job goes to the floppy disk after leaving the CPU be 0.1 (the probability a job goes to the hard disk after leaving the CPU be 0.9) and the probability a job returns to the CPU after leaving an I/O device be .875 (the number of CPU-I/O cycles has a geometric distribution starting at one with mean 8 cycles). If we let $r_1 = 1$, then $r_2 = 8$, $r_3 = 0.8$ and $r_4 = 7.2$. (These are the class values. Since there is one class per queue, the corresponding queue values are the

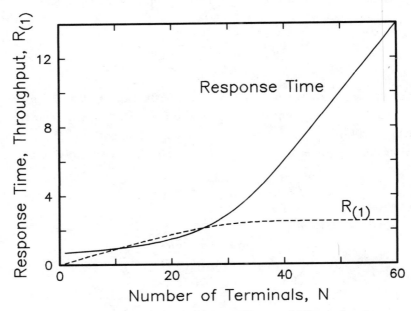

Figure 2.13 - Mean Response Time and Throughput

same.) Then for $n = 1$ from the first loop on m we get $Q_1(1) = 10$ seconds, $Q_2(1) = 50$ ms., $Q_3(1) = 220$ ms. and $Q_4(1) = 19$ ms. Next we get $R_{(1)}(1) = 0.09335$ jobs per second, $R_{(2)}(1) = 0.7468$ jobs per second, $R_{(3)}(1) = 0.07468$ jobs per second and $R_{(4)}(1) = 0.6721$ jobs per second. We also get $L_1(1) = 0.9335$ jobs, $L_2(1) = 0.0373$ jobs, $L_3(1) = 0.0164$ jobs and $L_4(1) = 0.0128$ jobs. For $n = 2$ from the first loop on m we get $Q_1(2) = 10$ seconds, $Q_2(2) = 51.87$ ms., $Q_3(2) = 223.6$ ms. and $Q_4(2) = 19.24$ ms. Proceeding to iterate on n until n reaches N, say 30, we get $Q_1(30) = 10$ seconds, $Q_2(30) = 302.6$ ms., $Q_3(30) = 364.7$ ms., $Q_4(30) = 27.52$ ms. and $R_{(1)}(30) = 2.324$ jobs per second. A mean response time, from issuing a command to receiving a response, will consist of 8 CPU mean queueing times (302.6 ms.), 0.8 floppy disk mean queueing times (364.7 ms.) and 7.2 hard disk mean queueing times (27.52 ms.) or 2.911 seconds. Figure 2.13 plots the throughput through the terminals and the mean response time, as a function of the number of terminals, N, as N ranges from 1 to 60.

2.2.3. General Product Form Networks

We have discussed in the last two sections the characteristics allowed in product form queueing networks that we believe are of the most interest in modeling computer communication systems. A variety of other characteristics are allowed by the product form solution. In terms of the individual queues, the most interesting characteristic we have ignored is service capacity dependent on queue length. Essentially arbitrary positive functions are allowed for service capacity, but the most interesting functions are those used to represent multiserver queues, e.g., for a two server queue, the capacity function would be 1 for queue length 1 and 2 for all queue lengths greater than 1. These functions significantly add to computational complexity for closed networks, but are otherwise easily considered.

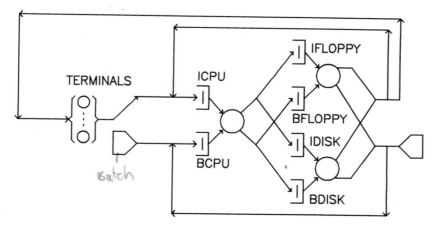

Figure 2.14 - Mixed Open and Closed Routing Chains

Another characteristic of interest is the mixing of open and closed routing chains in a single network, as illustrated in Figure 2.14. This illustrates adding a batch workload to our previous computer system model. Mixed networks are easily handled computationally; the solution of a mixed network can be transformed into the solution of a corresponding closed network.

Most of the remaining characteristics allowed in product form networks have seen little practical application. For an open routing chain, the arrival rates of sources need not be constant, but may be functions of the network or chain population. Constraints may be placed on the allowed populations in a network, resulting in a network which is neither closed nor open. Certain routing functions dependent on queue length and service capacity functions dependent on subnetwork populations are also allowed.

2.3. FURTHER READING

The most comprehensive collection of results on queueing models with tractable mathematical solution is found in Lavenberg and Sauer [12]. That work includes no derivations, however. Kleinrock Volume I [8] is an appropriate source of development of results for queues in isolation, and Sauer and Chandy [19] provide the most general development of results for product form networks which has been published so far.

CHAPTER 3

EXTENDED QUEUEING NETWORKS

Though mathematically tractable queueing networks are interesting in their own right, we find them more interesting as a basis for definition of models to be simulated. Queueing models provide an appropriate level of abstraction of systems that allows concise, yet understandable characterizations. However, even when we relax some of the assumptions imposed for the sake of mathematical analysis, e.g., assumptions about arrival and service time distributions, basic queueing networks are insufficient for representing a number of important system characteristics. Lacking are features for representing characteristics such as simultaneous resource possession, e.g., holding of buffers while using a link for transmission, parallelism and synchronization, e.g., generation of control messages and packetizing and reassembly of messages, and effects of protocols.

In this chapter we first define basic queueing networks of the same sort discussed in the last chapter, but this time define them from a simulation point of view, without regard to tractability of mathematical analysis. We next consider the functions and variables, in the sense of programming languages, which we consider necessary and their relationship to the network definition. These functions and variables typically depend on the state of the simulated system. Third, we define the most important extension to basic queueing networks, the "passive" queue. Passive queues provide a concise mechanism for representing simultaneous resource possession, e.g., possession of buffers and a link simultaneously. Simultaneous possession of logical resources is also part of many protocols, e.g., possession of a position in a window of a flow control mechanism while using a physical resource such as a communication link. Passive queues are also useful in instrumentation of a simulation model, e.g., to capture response times in a subnetwork. Finally, we discuss extensions useful for representing parallelism and synchronization.

Fully effective use of extended queueing network models depends on diagrams showing the network representation of the modeled system. As we define the elements of extended queueing networks, we will also define the diagram symbols for these elements. The most difficult part of modeling a system becomes the construction of model diagrams. This process requires understanding and abstraction of the modeled system. Then, with an appropriate software package such as RESQ, construction of the actual machine definition of the model is a mechanical translation process, translating the diagram to the machine definition and supplying numerical values. (Several research efforts are attempting to actually mechanize this translation.)

3.1. BASIC QUEUEING NETWORKS

What we call "basic" queueing networks are essentially the same as networks with the product form solution, but without requirements necessary for the product form, e.g., without the requirement that FCFS queues have exponential service time distributions. A basic queueing network consists of a set of jobs which visit queues and request service from the servers at those queues. The network may have sources for external arrivals of jobs and a sink for departure of jobs.

3.1.1. Active Queues

We refer to queues with servers as "active" queues. A job's activity is typically focused on the servers of active queues. A job typically has no interaction with other model elements while at an active queue. Each queue has one or more servers. A server belonging to one queue may not belong to another queue. A server may have a fixed service rate (capacity), as in the examples we have given so far. A server may instead have a service rate which is a function of the state of the queue, e.g., on the number of jobs at the queue. We will not make much use of such rate functions and will defer further discussion of them until we do make use of them.

Each queue has one or more classes. A class belonging to one queue may not belong to another queue. Multiple classes at a queue are useful to categorize jobs at the queue. The categorization may be used to distinguish routing of the jobs, to distinguish work demands (service requirements) of the jobs and/or to distinguish priorities. Jobs within a class may be further distinguished, e.g., by the "job variables" discussed in Section 3.2. A job arriving at a class demands a certain amount of work from a server of the queue. Examples of work demand could be number of bytes to be transmitted by a communication link, number of instructions to be executed by a processor, etc. Usually work demand will be characterized by a probability distribution or a numerical expression (which may involve probability distributions). In general, work demand is divided by service rate to obtain service time. The service rate is the amount of work the server can perform in one unit of time. In the usual case of fixed rate servers, the server may be assumed to have unit rate of service and work demand may be expressed as service time, as in all of our examples so far. Once a job is assigned a server it receives service until the work demand is satisfied or the job is preempted. However, once a job joins a class it remains part of that class until its work demand is satisfied, i.e., it remains part of the class while receiving service. Service may be preempted by arriving jobs or shared by other jobs, depending on the scheduling discipline.

Figure 3.1 - Active Queues
Single, Multiple, Infinite Server

Figure 3.1 shows the symbols we use for active queues, indicating the servers and classes. The servers are shown as circles, with braces indicating a collection of servers at one queue. The symbol for a class is intended to suggest a waiting line. In the special case of an "infinite" server queue, one with enough servers that there will never be waiting for servers, the class symbols are omitted.

3.1.2. Sources and Sink

A network may have one or more sources of jobs. Each source has an unlimited supply of jobs. The source emits jobs one at a time, with the time between emissions referred to as the "inter-arrival" time, or simply, "arrival" time. This time is usually specified by a probability distribution but may be specified by a general numerical expression. In basic networks the time between arrivals is completely determined by the arrival time value, but in extended networks additional control, including the ability to turn off sources, is available. This control is effected using the "chain variables" discussed in Section 3.2. Routing from sources is handled the same as routing from classes, as we discuss in the next section.

Only a single sink is necessary to provide for departures of jobs. In basic networks, a sink has no function other than as an exit point. In extended networks, a sink may assume implicit functions as needed.

SOURCE   SINK

Figure 3.2 - Source and Sink

Figure 3.2 shows the symbols for a source and a sink. Each symbol is a pentagon, with the only distinction being the direction of the arrow indicating the flow of jobs.

3.1.3. Routing and Routing Chains

We define routing in a (basic or extended) queueing network as being between elements categorized as "nodes." Classes, sources and the sink (if present) are all categorized as nodes. Queues are *not* categorized as nodes — the routing between queues is not defined directly but in terms of routing between classes. We will define a number of other types of nodes in the remaining sections of this chapter.

The nodes of the network, except for the sink, are partitioned into one or more "routing chains," or simply, "chains." The routing chains are disjoint except that several chains may be connected to the sink. The jobs of the network are also partitioned into these same chains, i.e., a job leaving a node in one chain may not go to a node in another chain. Normally the nodes of a chain are connected to each other, so that a job at one node of the chain can eventually get to another node of the chain unless it goes to the sink first. (The connection is not necessarily direct.) The nodes of a chain may be partitioned into disjoint subchains.

There are two basic types of chains, "closed" and "open." Closed chains have a fixed number of jobs (the "population") which remain among the nodes of the chain throughout the simulation. Open chains have a (usually) fluctuating number of jobs. Jobs leave the chain (and the network, simultaneously) by going to the sink. In a basic network, an open chain also has one or more sources for external arrival of jobs. In an extended network sources are not strictly necessary in an open chain since jobs initially placed in the chain may produce additional jobs by visiting split nodes, as discussed in Section 3.4. Jobs may be placed at nodes of open chains at the beginning of simulation, in addition to the jobs which will arrive from sources during the simulation. Figure 2.11 illustrates a network with two closed routing chains. Figure 2.13 illustrates a network with one closed routing chains and one open routing chain.

In a basic queueing network, routing decisions are usually limited to the fixed probabilities that we discussed in the last chapter, i.e., a job leaving one node selects among one or more possible destinations according to prespecified probabilities. In an extended network other decision mechanisms are possible, as we discuss in the next section.

3.2. NETWORK VARIABLES AND FUNCTIONS

One necessary extension to basic queueing networks is the provision of functions and variables which provide and maintain data about the simulated system and its elements. This data may then be used may be used in expressions for arrival times, service times, priorities, routing and other model characteristics to dynamically specify these characteristics.

There are three basic categories of variables required, with the different categories of variables distinguished by their associations with different network elements. (1) Job variables are used to store data associated with individual jobs. (2) Chain variables are used to store data associated with individual routing chains. (3) Global variables are used for data associated with subnetworks or the entire network.

Within these categories one may further distinguish different data types, e.g., Boolean, fixed point, floating point, or character strings, but floating point data can be used to represent Boolean and fixed point data and is usually sufficient. We assume that only floating point data is provided.

There are two categories of functions needed: distribution functions which return samples from specified probability distributions and status functions which return information such as the current queue length at a particular queue.

3.2.1. Variable Declaration, Naming and Assignment

In principal all three categories of variables can be treated similarly to variables in programming languages. The simulation language provides for declaration of the variable names (including array extents), for specification of their category (job, chain or global), for initialization of values and for assignment. In practice, global variables are used as programming language variables and this general treatment is appropriate to global variables. However, job and chain variables are used much more specifically. The general treatment of job and chain variables leads to potential confusion of the simulation language user (e.g., a variable is not recognized as belonging to a particular category unless a special syntax or naming convention is used). The general treatment of job variables also leads to implementation efficiency problems, since there will be many instances of the variables. For these reasons we prefer restrictive treatment of job and chain variables and general treatment of global variables.

The characteristics of the three categories of variables, in terms of applications, declarations and naming conventions, will be discussed in the following three subsections. Assignment to variables of any of the three categories is performed at "set nodes." A set node is defined to have one or more assignment statements in the programming language sense. A job

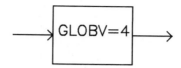

Figure 3.3 - Set Node

visiting a set node causes the assignment statements associated with that set node to be performed. In our diagrams we will show set nodes as rectangles, with the assignment statements shown within the set node where practical. Figure 3.3 gives an example.

3.2.2. Job Variables

We assume that job variables consist of a single vector named "JV," with each job having its own vector, but all vectors having the same number of elements. The entire vector is initialized to zeroes when a job is placed in the network at the beginning of simulation or generated by a source. (For jobs generated by fission or split nodes, the vector of the generated job receives the same values as the generating job, as discussed in Section 2.4.)

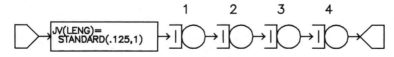

Figure 3.4 - Series Queues with Interdependence

An important application of job variables is avoidance of the independence assumption discussed in Section 2.2. If a value representing message length is stored in a job variable, then this value may be used in calculating service time, i.e., by dividing by the link capacity and adding the propagation delay. Consider the network of Figure 3.4, with four queues in series.

Let us suppose the propagation delay is negligible, that the arrival times have an exponential distribution with mean 0.25 second ($\lambda = 4$ jobs per second) and that the message lengths have an exponential distribution with mean length 300 bits, and that the link capacities are 2400 baud. Then $S = 0.125$ second for each queue and $\rho = 0.5$ for each queue. If we make the independence assumption, we would expect L to be 1 for each queue and Q to be 0.25 second for each queue. The set node in Figure 3.4 assumes that "leng" is a predefined constant indicating which element of JV is to be used to store the message length. The distribution function "standard(.125,1)" results in the desired exponential distribution, as we discuss in Section 3.2.5 below. We simulated this model using a job variable to avoid the independence assumption (using RESQ). For a run of 2500 simulated seconds we obtained the following point estimates and confidence intervals at a 90% level of confidence:

m	L		Q	(seconds)
1	1.01	(0.96,1.05)	0.25	(0.24,0.26)
2	1.07	(1.03,1.11)	0.27	(0.26,0.28)
3	1.25	(1.20,1.31)	0.31	(0.30,0.32)
4	1.40	(1.34,1.46)	0.35	(0.34,0.36)

(Confidence intervals provide an estimate of accuracy of simulation results. We will discuss confidence interval methods briefly in Chapter 4 and cite references there.) Clearly, as originally observed by Kleinrock, the independence assumption is not appropriate for this model.

3.2.3. Chain Variables

Chain variables have only one unique function, to control the rates of sources of the chains. Though chain variables can be used for other purposes, it will usually be more appropriate to use global variables for these purposes. We assume that chain variables consist of a single vector named "CV," with each chain having its own vector, but all vectors having the same number of elements. The entire vector is initialized to ones when simulation begins.

Only CV(0) affects sources. If CV(0) for an open chain is positive, samples from the arrival time distributions are divided by CV(0) to obtain actual interarrival times, i.e., CV(0) acts as a scaling factor for source arrival rates. If CV(0) is positive and is changed to another positive value, pending arrivals for that chain are rescheduled. The new time until an arrival is obtained by multiplying the old time until the arrival by the old value of CV(0) and dividing that result by the new value of CV(0). Setting CV(0) to 0 (or a negative value) shuts off all sources for that chain; any pending source arrivals for the chain are cancelled and no new arrivals will be scheduled, even if CV(0) should later become positive.

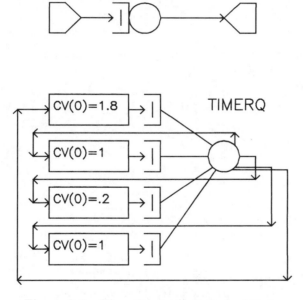

Figure 3.5 - Time Dependent Arrival Rates

As an example of the use of CV(0) to change arrival rates, consider a link where the arrival rates vary according to a pattern associated with the number of minutes past the hour. Because of the nature of the users of the link, the first 15 minutes of the hour has a relatively high arrival rate, 7.2 messages per second. The second 15 minutes have a moderate arrival rate, 4 messages per second, the third 15 minutes of the hour have a low arrival rate, 0.8 messages per second, and the last 15 minutes have a moderate rate again, 4 messages per second. Thus the average arrival rate over the hour is 4 messages per second. Let us suppose that in each of these fifteen minute periods the arrival times have an exponential distribution, i.e., in the first 15 minutes of the hour the time between arrivals has an exponential distribution with mean 0.138 seconds. Let the service times have an exponential distribution with mean 0.125 seconds. If we assumed this system to be an M/M/1 queue with $\lambda = 4$, then we would have $\rho = 0.5$, $L = 1$ and $Q = 0.25$ seconds.

Figure 3.5 shows an extended queueing network representation for this example. The top part of the figure shows the subchain consisting of source, queue and its connection to the sink. The bottom part of the figure shows a subchain consisting of the set nodes used to change $CV(0)$ and a queue which times the 15 minute intervals. There is a single job alternating between set nodes and classes with 15 minute times representing the above periods. We simulated this model for 25 independent one hour periods and, as expected, obtained the value 0.50 for ρ, with confidence interval (0.496,0.500) at a 90% level of confidence. However, we obtained the value 2.71 for L, with confidence interval (2.54,2.88) and the value 0.68 seconds for Q, with confidence interval (0.64,0.72). Thus the fluctuating arrival rate causes dramatic deterioration of performance as averaged over the hour.

3.2.4. Global Variables

Job variables are local to individual jobs and not accessible by other jobs. Chain variables are local to individual chains and not accessible by jobs in other chains. In addition to these special variables, we also need variables accessible by all jobs, regardless of chain. Since these variables are not local to jobs or chains, we refer to them as "global" variables. They have naming conventions as in programming languages, are declared and initialized as in programming languages and are assigned values in assignment statements of set nodes. There are two additional points to be made:

- In a language such as RESQ which allows macro definition of subnetworks, there should be provision for "global" variables which are local to subnetworks (but global to jobs and chains). The conventions for these subnetwork global variables naturally follow those of block structured programming languages (e.g., Algol, Pascal and PL/I). We will make frequent use of such macro definitions and global variables defined within the macro definitions in our examples in Chapters 5, 6 and 7.

• It is useful to have global variables with special meanings known to both the simulation program and the modeler. Most important is a "clock" variable, i.e., one that contains the current simulated time. (As an alternative to special global variables, one could instead define status functions without arguments. This may even be preferable for values such as simulated time that should not be modified by the model. However, other values may be modified by both the simulation program and the model and are appropriately defined as special global variables.)

3.2.5. Distribution Functions

When one has little information about random values other than mean values, then it is reasonable to arbitrarily assume that the random values have a distribution which is completely specified by the mean, e.g., the exponential distribution. When one has more information, and that information indicates that the exponential distribution is not an appropriate representation, then one should use a representation which includes that information. For example, if one knows standard deviations are substantially different from mean values (with the exponential distribution the standard deviation equals the mean), one should include standard deviations in the model. All simulation languages have basic facilities for defining probability distributions. Many other distributions can be obtained by combining these basic facilities in arithmetic expressions. We now summarize the basic facilities we find appropriate in RESQ.

The coefficient of variation is defined as the standard deviation divided by the mean. RESQ provides a standardized distribution form which is completely specified by the mean and coefficient of variation and which is expedient for simulation and confidence interval estimation. The STANDARD distribution will often be sufficient. However, if the user has additional information then the user may wish to try to fit the distribution more precisely. The DISCRETE distribution provides a direct mechanism for doing this in which the distribution is defined by a table of values and associated probabilities. This may be appropriate to empirically obtained data. If the DISCRETE distribution is not appropriate or convenient, then a continuous distribution, either the BE (Branching Erlang) or UNIFORM distribution, will usually be appropriate. Since the STANDARD distribution is a combination of these two, we consider them first.

BE Distribution. A number of distribution forms can be grouped together as representatives of the *method of exponential stages.* Perhaps the best known of these are the Erlang distribution, the hypoexponential distribution and the hyperexponential distribution. The branching Erlang (BE) distribution is less well known but includes all three of the above distributions and many other distributions as special cases. Figure 3.6 illustrates the branching Erlang form.

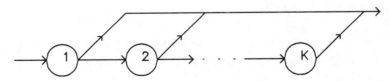

Figure 3.6 - BE (Branching Erlang) Distribution

The BE distribution may be thought of as consisting of K exponential stages (which are represented by circles in the figure). Stage i, $i = 1,...,K$, has a mean (exponential time) m_i and a "branching" probability (to be described shortly) p_i. A sample from the distribution consists of the sum of (independent) samples from stages 1 to k where k is between 1 and K and selected by the following rule: With probability p_1, k is chosen to be 1, with probability $(1 - p_1)p_2$, k is chosen to be 2, ... and with probability $(1 - p_1)(1 - p_2)...(1 - p_{K-1})$, k is chosen to be K. In other words, p_i is the probability of branching past the stages after stage i. Note that p_K is identically 1. The mean, M, of the BE distribution is given by

$$M = \sum_{k=1}^{K} (1 - p_1)(1 - p_2)...(1 - p_{k-1})p_k \sum_{i=1}^{k} m_i$$

and the coefficient of variation, C, is given by

$$C = \frac{\sqrt{\sum_{k=1}^{K} (1-p_1)(1-p_2)...(1-p_{k-1})p_k \left[\sum_{i=1}^{k} m_i^2 + \left(\sum_{i=1}^{k} m_i \right)^2 \right]} - M^2}{M}$$

(Since we will no longer be enumerating classes, we will no longer use C for the number of classes.)

The BE distribution reduces to the exponential distribution if we set p_1 to 1 and m_1 to M where M is the mean of the distribution. The BE distribution reduces to the Erlang distribution if we set p_i to zero for all i other than K and set m_i to M/K. The hypoexponential distribution is a generalization of the Erlang distribution which does not require equality of the stage means $\{m_i\}$. A 2 stage hyperexponential distribution can be thought of as a choice of an exponential distribution with mean m_1 with probability q and a choice of an exponential distribution with mean m_2 otherwise. Without loss of generality we may assume $m_1 < m_2$. Then the BE distribution with 2 stages and the corresponding stage means is equivalent to the hyperexponential if we set p_1 to $q + (1 - q)m_1/m_2$. (If we wish to have the classical representation of hyperexponential service times at a queue we can accomplish this by having two classes with exponential distributions with means m_1 and m_2 and routing a job to the first class with probability q and to the second class otherwise.)

UNIFORM Distribution. The classical uniform distribution is one with uniform (positive) probability density over an interval (l, u) and zero density elsewhere. The uniform distribution provided by RESQ is a generalization of the classical form in that it allows several intervals instead of just one. The mean of the classical uniform distribution is given by

$$M = \frac{l + u}{2}$$

and the coefficient of variation is

$$C = \frac{u - l}{(l + u)\sqrt{3}}.$$

Alternatively, if we are given the mean and coefficient of variation,

$$u = M(1 + C\sqrt{3})$$

and

$$l = 2M - u.$$

STANDARD Distribution. In many circumstances one is satisfied by specifying a distribution by mean and coefficient of variation. RESQ includes a pragmatically chosen collection of distributions so specified. The distribution used will have mean M and coefficient of variation C where the specific form is chosen according to the value of C. If $C = 0$, then the constant value M is used. If $0 < C < .5$, then the classical uniform form is used. If $.5 \leq C < 1$, then the BE distribution is used with

$$K = \text{ceil}(C^{-2}),$$

$$p_1 = \frac{2KC^2 + K - 2 - \sqrt{K^2 + 4 - 4KC^2}}{(K-1)2(C^2 + 1)}$$

$$p_2 = \ldots = p_{K-1} = 0$$

and

$$m_1 = \ldots = m_K = M/(K - p_1(K-1)).$$

Here "ceil" is the ceiling function, i.e., it returns the next larger integer if its argument is not an integer and returns its argument otherwise. Note that this results in the Erlang distribution for $C = .5$, $\sqrt{3}$ and $\sqrt{2}$. If $C = 1$ the exponential distribution is used and if $C > 1$ the hyperexponential distribution specified is used with $K = 2$,

$$p_1 = C^2\left(1 - \sqrt{1 - \frac{2}{1 + C^2}}\right),$$

$$m_1 = \frac{M}{1 + \sqrt{1 - \frac{2}{1 + C^2}}}$$

and

$$m_2 = \frac{M}{1 - \sqrt{1 - \frac{2}{1 + C^2}}}.$$

The discontinuity here, using the classical uniform distribution for small coefficient of variation and the BE distribution for larger coefficient of variation, is due to our general preference for the BE distribution tempered by the computational expense of simulating the BE distribution for small coefficient of variation. (The number of BE stages, and thus computational expense, becomes large with small coefficient of variation.)

3.2.6. Routing Predicates

In basic queueing networks routing decisions are made strictly according to fixed probabilities. (In product form networks, limited forms of probabilities dependent on queue lengths are permitted.) However, a more expressive mechanism, analogous to "IF THEN" statements in programming languages, is needed in extended queueing networks. As an alternative to associating a probability with a (directed) path between nodes, a "predicate," i.e., a Boolean function, may be associated with a path between nodes. The predicate has either a true or false value dependent on network variables and functions. For example, a possible predicate is "IF(JV(LENG)<256)". If, when a path is being considered for the routing of a job, the predicate has a true value, that path is taken.

3.2.7. Status Functions

In routing predicates especially, but also in other uses of expressions, the model must be able to determine characteristics of system state. For example, a routing predicate may depend on whether there are servers available at a queue (and if so, how many), on total queue length for all classes of a queue and/or queue length at a specific class. These three examples are the most important status functions for the network elements we have defined so far. Additional functions are required to take full advantage of the passive queues and other elements defined in the remainder of this chapter.

3.3. PASSIVE QUEUES

The passive queue is the most important extension to the basic queueing network. A job typically acquires units of resources represented by passive queues and simply (passively) holds these resource units while visiting active queues and other model elements. The job explicitly releases or destroys the resource units when they are no longer needed. The resources represented by active queues are the focus of the job's activities, but without the passive queue resources these active queue resources are not usable. For example, before a message can be transmitted on a communication link, there must be a buffer available at the receiving end to store the incoming message. Buffers are resources typically represented by passive queues. Similarly, a passive queue representing memory may be appropriately added to the computer system models of Section 2.2. Passive queues representing I/O channels and/or device controllers might also be appropriately added to those or similar models. Besides these representations of simultaneous possession of physical resources, passive queues are key to the representations of simultaneous possession of logical resources, as we will illustrate thoroughly in Chapter 6. We will also depend on passive queues as instrumentation devices, primarily for measuring response times. The queueing time for a passive queue is defined as the time between a job's request for resource units and that job's freeing or destroying of the resource units.

The resource units represented by a passive queue are assumed to be homogeneous. The resource units are called "tokens." The tokens of a passive queue correspond to the servers of an active queue. A passive queue consists of a pool of tokens to be allocated to jobs and a set of nodes which operate on that pool and the jobs holding tokens. Figure 3.7 shows the diagram symbols used to represent passive queues.

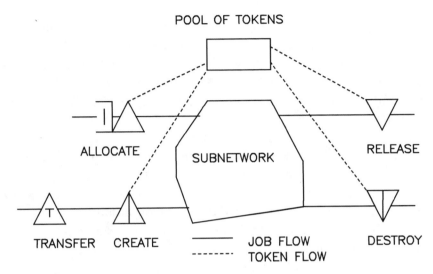

Figure 3.7 - Passive Queue

The primary nodes of passive queues are called "allocate" nodes. Allocate nodes correspond to the classes of active queues. A job arriving at an allocate node requests possession of a number of the queue's tokens. This number may be a constant, a sample from a probability distribution, an expression based on job, chain or global variables, etc. If the tokens requested are not available for this job, the job waits at the allocate node. Scheduling of allocations will usually be either FCFS or non-preemptive priority, but other scheduling disciplines are possible. As soon as the tokens are allocated, the job is allowed to visit other nodes of the network. However, as long as the job waits for or possesses tokens of a given passive queue, it is considered to be associated with that queue and the allocate node where it obtained tokens, e.g., it is counted in the queue lengths for the queue and allocate node.

When a job visits a "release" node associated with a particular passive queue, it instantaneously returns to the pool of tokens all tokens which it holds. The job is no longer associated with the queue, e.g., the queueing time ends, and the job proceeds without delay. When a job visits a release node associated with a particular passive queue without holding tokens of that queue, there is no effect on the job or queue. Fusion nodes (Section 3.4) and the sink may have the effect of releasing tokens.

When a job visits a "destroy" node associated with a particular passive queue, it instantaneously destroys all tokens which it holds. The job is no longer associated with the queue, e.g., the queueing time ends, and the job proceeds without delay. When a job visits a destroy node associated with a particular passive queue without holding tokens of that queue, there is no effect on the job or queue.

"Create" nodes are used by a job to add new tokens to a pool of tokens, usually to complement the effects of a destroy node. A job visiting a create node may or may not hold tokens of that queue, the effect is the same in either case. A visit to a create node is instantaneous as far as simulated time is concerned. In representing communication protocols and similar mechanisms, it is often the case that a job will destroy tokens and later either create tokens itself or have another job create tokens. This is effectively a release of tokens, but can be used to represent delays in notification of token availability (e.g., the transmission delay for an acknowledgement).

"Transfer" nodes are used to transfer tokens between related jobs, as discussed in the following section.

3.4. SPLIT, FISSION AND FUSION NODES

Split nodes allow a job to produce additional independent jobs. Split nodes are useful in representing bulk arrival mechanisms and in representing control messages (e.g., acknowledgements) in communication system protocols. A split node has one entrance, an exit for the job that entered and an additional exit for each new job to be produced. The newly produced jobs are given the same job variable values as the existing job. The newly produced jobs do not possess tokens, whether or not the existing job possessed tokens. A visit to a split node is instantaneous, as far as simulated time is concerned.

Figure 3.8 - Split, Fission and Fusion Nodes

Fission nodes allow a job to produce additional jobs dependent on the existing job. Fusion nodes allow for the destruction of the newly produced jobs in a coordinated manner. Fission and fusion nodes are usually used together in pairs. Fission and fusion nodes are useful for representing synchronized processes (tasks) occurring in operating systems. Similarly, fission and fusion nodes are useful for representing parallel physical activities representing a single logical activity, for example transmission of a message across a communication network as a collection of packets.

A fission node has one entrance, an exit for the existing job (referred to as the "parent"), and an additional exit for each new job to be produced. The produced jobs are referred to as "children." Children may themselves enter fission nodes, thus producing hierarchies of jobs. Children are given the same job variable values as the parent. The children do not possess tokens, whether or not the parent does. A visit to a fission node is instantaneous, as far as simulated time is concerned. Jobs are not allowed to leave the network (i.e., by going to the sink) as long as they have relatives (parents or children). This is not the case with jobs going through a split node, since split jobs are not related.

A fusion node provides a place for jobs to wait for related jobs (parents or children). A fusion node has no effect on jobs without relatives. Such jobs pass through a fusion node without delay or other effect. No more than one job of a "family" can stay at a fusion node. If a job arrives at a fusion node and it has relatives, but none of its relatives are at this particular fusion node, it waits at the fusion nodes. When a job arrives at fusion node and it has a relative at this particular fusion node, two things can happen, depending on the relationship between the jobs. If one is the parent and the other is a child, then the offspring is destroyed. If both are children, the one that was produced last is destroyed. Before a child is destroyed, any tokens it holds are released. After destruction of one job, if the other job has no remaining relatives, it proceeds from the exit of the fusion node. If the other job still has other relatives, it waits at the fusion node for another relative to arrive.

"Transfer" nodes are used to transfer tokens between parent and child. The transfer may be in either direction, but is always initiated by the child. When a child is generated at a fission node, it possesses no tokens of passive queues. A transfer node allows a child to request transfer of its parent's tokens of a particular passive queue. This will typically, but not necessarily, occur immediately after the child is generated. If a child acquires tokens, through either allocate or transfer nodes, and does not dispose of them prior to going to a fusion node, the tokens will be released as part of the fusion operation. A transfer node also allows a child to transfer all of its tokens of a particular passive queue back to its parent.

As already mentioned, a child may go to a fission node to produce its own children. There are two rules which must be kept in mind:

1. Whenever a job visits a fission node, it produces its immediate descendent, i.e., a job can never directly produce grandchildren.
2. Related jobs more than one generation apart, e.g., grandparents and grandchildren, may not be present at the same fusion node.

An immediate consequence of these rules is that it is usually necessary to have (at least one) separate pair of fission and fusion nodes for every generation of jobs that is to be produced.

Figure 3.9 illustrates an abstract set of fission and fusion nodes which might be tailored to a variety of purposes. For example, suppose a communication network is such that messages must be broken into packets for

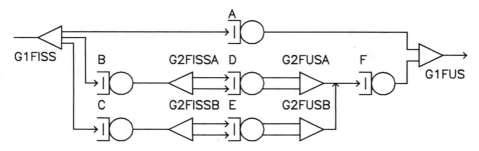

Figure 3.9 - Nesting of Fission and Fusion Nodes

transmission and must be broken into sub-packets for transmission across certain links. Further, a message consists of exactly two packets and a packet consists of exactly two sub-packets. Node G1FISS (generation 1 fission) in the figure could represent breaking the message into packets. Since a job that enters G1FISS cannot directly generate grandchildren, it generates two children, representing the packets. Queue A would be eliminated in this case and the jobs that enter G1FISS would go directly to G1FUSE. The children leaving G1FISS would be transmitted across the portion of the network allowing full packets, e.g., queues B and C in the figure. Then they reach G2FISSA and G2FISSB, where they produce children to represent breaking the packets into sub-packets. A child represents one sub-packet and a grandchild represents the other. After transmission across the portion of the network requiring sub-packets, e.g., queues D and E in the figure, a child and grandchild can reunite at the generation 2 fusion nodes to represent assembling the sub-packets into packets. The child (packet) then proceeds further across the network, e.g., through queue F in the figure to the generation 1 fusion node. When both children have reached the fusion node, their parent (representing the reassembled message) leaves the fusion node.

CHAPTER 4

THE RESEARCH QUEUEING PACKAGE (RESQ)

In order to effectively use queueing networks as performance models, appropriate software is necessary for definition of the networks to be solved, for solution of the networks (by numerical or simulation methods) and for examination of the performance measures obtained. The Research Queueing Package (RESQ) which we have constructed is an example of such software for simulation of extended queueing networks. Using a tool such as RESQ, construction of simulation models becomes a relatively effortless process.

In this book, our focus is on simulation methodology for computer communication systems and we use diagrams and informal descriptions to convey the use of extended queueing network models. However, we wish to put our examples on more concrete footing by giving formal definitions of our models. The model definitions are the ones used with RESQ, so we wish that the reader have enough familiarity with RESQ conventions that RESQ model definitions used in our examples will be understandable. Ambiguities in the diagrams and informal descriptions are resolved in the formal definitions. These definitions may be readily translated to the definitions used with other tools that support equivalent extended queueing network models.

Simulation methodology involves more than model definition. In particular, it involves statistical analysis of simulation outputs and determination of appropriate simulation run lengths. RESQ is especially strong in this area, so discussion of RESQ gives us an appropriate basis for discussion of these issues, both in terms of software capabilities and application to particular simulations. In Section 4.1 we discuss simulation specific issues of analyzing simulation output, initializing the simulation, and determining run length.

The remainder of this chapter provides an overview of RESQ as it pertains to this book. For more thorough discussion, see the references in the Bibliography. In Section 4.2 we discuss the basic syntax and semantics of network definition with RESQ. In Section 4.3 we discuss the RESQ capabilities for macro definitions of subnetworks. Both of these sections are essentially independent of solution method, though much of the discussion applies only to simulation.

4.1. SIMULATION SPECIFIC ISSUES

There are two primary issues we wish to address, the estimation of accuracy of simulation performance measures obtained from simulations and the determination of simulation run length. An additional issue which we consider part of the accuracy issue is the initialization of simulations.

4.1.1. Confidence Intervals

Simulation, as we apply it, inherently involves statistical variability due to the use of (pseudo-) random number streams. This variability is not a problem with numerical solutions, where we obtain exact values for model performance measures (within the limits of numerical accuracy). With either simulation or numerical solutions, we would like to think that our main source of errors in results is inaccuracy of representation of a system, i.e., our model ignores some system characteristic which significantly impacts performance. However, if simulation is improperly used, errors due to statistical variability may dominate errors due to model inaccuracies.

The standard statistical method for estimating the accuracy of simulation results is to compute a "confidence interval." In addition to the usual "point estimate" p for some performance measure (say throughput), an interval estimate $(p-\delta, p+\delta)$ is computed at a specified "confidence level," e.g., 90%. We expect the true value of the performance measure to be contained in the computed interval most of the time, e.g., 90%, but know that the true value may fall outside of the interval (but, hopefully, near the interval).

Computing confidence intervals for simulation results is not an easy matter, and research in the area continues. However, a number of approaches are of considerable practical value. RESQ implements three of these, each with its own advantages and disadvantages, and allows the user to select the one most appropriate to the problem at hand. The three methods are the classical method of "independent replications," the relatively recent "regenerative" method and the very recent "spectral" method. The implementations are designed to be transparent to the user, so that the user need not understand the statistical bases for the methods nor need the user provide many parameters. This contrasts sharply with most simulation languages, which provide no support at all for confidence interval estimation. Most users will not go to the trouble of programming their own output analysis routines and will be vulnerable to relying on results with substantial inaccuracies due to statistical variability.

Independent replications. Much of classical statistics depends on data items being independent and identically distributed. The obvious items of data for analysis in simulations of queueing networks will not have this property, e.g., the length of one response time is likely to be significantly related to the lengths of previous response times. The basis of the method of independent replications is to obtain independent and identically distributed groups of data by replicating (repeating) simulation runs. Each replication begins with the same initial conditions, except for the random number streams, and each replication has the same length, so the results from the replications are independent and identically distributed. For example, in the simulation of the queue with arrival rate dependent on the time past the hour (Figure 3.5), we repeated the simulation 25 times. Each simulation began with the queue empty at the beginning of the hour. The method of independent replications is quite appropriate to a problem of this sort, where we recognize and accept the transient behavior of the system (in this case the arrival rates dependent on simulated time).

Usually, however, we are interested in equilibrium behavior, the behavior we would expect to observe after a run of indefinite length. Independent replications is not well suited to this sort of problem for two reasons. First, the behavior of the system depends on the initial state of the system until the simulation has run long enough for the effects of the choice of initial state to be effectively masked. This problem can be alleviated somewhat by discarding an initial portion of each replication, but one must accept the computational costs of each of these discarded initial portions. Second, one must determine how long each replication should be, and this is a difficult problem without analysis of the characteristics of individual replications.

The Regenerative Method.   In many queueing networks it is possible to identify portions of a single simulation run that are independent and identically distributed.   For example, in the $M/G/1$ queue, periods of simulation between returns to the state where the system is empty (and the server is idle) are independent and identically distributed because of the memoryless property of the exponential interarrival time distribution.   A state such as the empty state in the $M/G/1$ queue is called a "regeneration" state and the periods between returns to the regeneration state are called regeneration "cycles."   All of the queueing systems discussed in Chapter 2 are regenerative systems, and so are many of the other systems we discuss.   For example, in the central server model with terminals of Figure 2.9, the state with all of the jobs at the terminals is a regeneration state.   Identification of regeneration states usually depends on the memoryless property of the exponential distribution.   It is for this reason that we advocate that (when appropriate) the Branching Erlang distribution be used for representing non-exponential service and arrival times.   The exponential stages of the Branching Erlang form may be used to identify regeneration states.

There are two principal limitations in using the regenerative method. First, the method only applies to systems with a regenerative structure. Though the extended queueing network definitions we have given are made with the intent of preserving regenerative structure, where possible, the extensions will eliminate regenerative structure in many cases. Second, even though a model regenerates in principle, a model may not return to the regeneration state in a simulation of reasonable length. Even if the simulation does return to the regeneration state a few times, this will not be sufficient for the statistical analysis to be valid.

The Spectral Method.   The spectral method does not depend on independent and identically distributed data items.   Rather, it explicitly takes into consideration the correlations between successive items in the analysis of the data.   Heidelberger and Welch [HEID81] describe the spectral method as follows. "An estimate of the variance is obtained by estimating the spectral density at zero frequency. This estimation is accomplished through a regression analysis of the logarithm of the averaged periodogram." The spectral method applies to equilibrium behavior of general extended queueing networks and is very easy to use. The principle problem with the spectral method is that it only applies easily to discrete items of data, i.e., it does not apply easily to time averaged data items such as utilization or queue length. In RESQ, the spectral method implementation provides confidence intervals for mean queueing times and queueing time distribution points only.

4.1.2. Stopping Rules

A common approach to determining simulation run lengths is to simply specify a run length in advance, e.g., to say the simulation will run for one simulated hour. However, if confidence intervals are available from a single run method (e.g., the regenerative method or the spectral method), then these may be used in an automated procedure where the specification given by the user is the required accuracy of the simulation results rather than an arbitrarily chosen run length. For example, the specification might be that the relative width of the confidence interval for some mean queueing time be less than 10%, i.e., if p is the mean queueing time value and (l,u) is the confidence interval, then the stopping criterion is that $(u-l)/p$ be no greater than 0.10.

Such an automated run length determination is usually implemented as a sequential procedure, where the simulation runs for a period of length specified by the user. If the accuracy criteria are satisfied, then the simulation terminates. If the criteria are not satisfied, then the simulation continues for one or more additional periods until the criteria are satisfied or the CPU budget for this run is exhausted. Sequential procedures should be used in a conservative manner, i.e., the period lengths should be specified that there be only a few, relatively long periods, not many short periods.

4.2. NETWORK DEFINITION

The RESQ user may define a network interactively with a prompter that leads the user through a network definition. Alternately, the user may provide a file giving the network definition, analogous to a file giving a program definition for a compiler. Such a file has the same syntax as the interactive dialogue, i.e., it includes both prompts and replies. For this reason it is called a "dialogue" file. The primary difference between the two modes is that the interactive mode has extra lines, prompts which receive no reply, which are necessary to terminate sections of interactive dialogue but are superfluous in dialogue file mode.

Users may switch freely between modes, e.g., while in interactive mode a user may reply "edit" to edit a dialogue file transcript of the network definition so far. Such editing may consist of minor corrections or whole-sale corrections. If the RESQ translator is given an incomplete dialogue file, it will automatically enter the interactive mode after it has parsed the incomplete file.

Our examples will be dialogue files which only include the portions of dialogue appropriate to the model at hand. Most lines in the files consist of a string of upper case characters followed by a colon (":") and a string of mixed case characters (primarily lower case characters). The upper case string and colon would be a prompt in interactive mode and the mixed case string would be the reply.

The common syntax between the two modes forces a fairly rigid sequence of sections in the dialogue file. There is an initial section declaring the solution method (numerical or simulation), parameters, identifiers representing constant values and variables. Then there is a section for declaration of macro definitions of queues and definitions of the queues themselves. The next section is for definition of other nodes not associated with queues, set nodes, split nodes, fission and fusion nodes. Following that are sections for declaration of subnetwork macros, which we call "submodels," and invocation of those macros. The final part of the network definition is the definition of routing chains. With simulation there is also a simulation specific section following the network definition.

We now use a sample dialogue file to illustrate the syntax and structure of the dialogues. This example illustrates a subset of dialogue characteristics. The file is for simulation of the network of Figure 2.6 without making

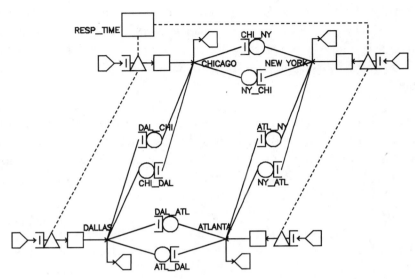

Figure 4.1 - Network without Independence Assumption

the independence assumption. See Figure 4.1. In addition to the elements shown in that figure, set nodes are used to set job variables for message destinations and lengths, and a passive queue is used to measure response times. The first major portion of dialogue establishes the model name, the solution method, parameters, constants and variables.

```
MODEL:chap4m1
   METHOD:simulation
   NUMERIC PARAMETERS:mean_leng /*mean message length*/
   DISTRIBUTION PARAMETERS:arrivl_tim /*arrival_times*/
   NUMERIC IDENTIFIERS:NY Atl Dal Chi
      NY:1
      ATL:2
      DAL:3
      CHI:4
   NUMERIC IDENTIFIERS:msg_dest msg_leng
      MSG_DEST:0 /*JV(0) to be used to store destination*/
      MSG_LENG:1 /*JV(1) to be used to store length    */
   DISTRIBUTION IDENTIFIERS:msg_l_dist /*message length */
      MSG_L_DIST:standard(mean_leng,1) /*exponential    */
   MAX JV:1 /*maximum subscript*/
```

(If global variables were being declared for this model, declaration and initialization would occur here, with syntax similar to the declaration of constants, i.e., the numeric and distribution identifiers.) Next are a macro definition of an active queue for representing links,

```
QUEUE TYPE:basic_link
   NUMERIC PARAMETERS:prop_delay
   NODE PARAMETERS:class_name
   TYPE:fcfs /*special case of active queue type*/
   CLASS LIST:class_name
      SERVICE TIMES:standard(jv(msg_leng)/9600+prop_delay,0)
END OF QUEUE TYPE BASIC_LINK
```

and 8 invocations of this macro definition which define the link queues.

```
QUEUE:NY_Atl_q
   TYPE:basic_link        /*invocation of user defined queue type */
   PROP_DELAY:.00408      /*using invocation form with matching of*/
   CLASS_NAME:NY_Atl      /*parameter names and values           */
QUEUE:Atl_Dal_q
   TYPE:basic_link: .00377; Atl_Dal /*positional invocation form*/
QUEUE:Dal_Chi_q
   TYPE:basic_link: .00423; Dal_Chi
QUEUE:Chi_NY_q
   TYPE:basic_link: .00377; Chi_NY
QUEUE:Atl_NY_q
   TYPE:basic_link: .00408; Atl_NY
QUEUE:Dal_Atl_q
   TYPE:basic_link: .00377; Dal_Atl
QUEUE:Chi_Dal_q
   TYPE:basic_link: .00423; Chi_Dal
QUEUE:NY_Chi_q
   TYPE:basic_link: .00377; NY_Chi
```

We then define a passive queue for measuring response times.

```
QUEUE:resp_time
   TYPE:passive
   TOKENS:2147483647    /* "infinity" -- 2**31-1 */
   DSPL:fcfs
   ALLOCATE NODE LIST:NY_r_t Atl_r_t Dal_r_t Chi_r_t
      NUMBERS OF TOKENS TO ALLOCATE:1
```

(The tokens will be released by the sink.) For each source there is a set node which determines the destination and message length and stores these in the appropriate job variables.

```
SET NODES:set_NY
ASSIGNMENT LIST:jv(msg_dest)=discrete(Atl,1/3;Dal,1/3;Chi,1/3) ++
               jv(msg_leng)=msg_l_dist
SET NODES:set_Atl
ASSIGNMENT LIST:jv(msg_dest)=discrete(NY,1/3;Dal,1/3;Chi,1/3)  ++
               jv(msg_leng)=msg_l_dist
SET NODES:set_Dal
ASSIGNMENT LIST:jv(msg_dest)=discrete(NY,1/3;Atl,1/3;Chi,1/3)  ++
               jv(msg_leng)=msg_l_dist
SET NODES:set_Chi
ASSIGNMENT LIST:jv(msg_dest)=discrete(NY,1/3;Atl,1/3;Dal,1/3)  ++
               jv(msg_leng)=msg_l_dist
```

The final portion of the network proper is the definition of routing, including declaration of sources.

```
CHAIN:c
  TYPE:open
  SOURCE LIST:New_York Atlanta Dallas Chicago
  ARRIVAL TIMES:arrivl_tim
  SOURCE LIST:New_York Atlanta Dallas Chicago
  ARRIVAL TIMES:arrivl_tim
  :New_York->NY_r_t->set_NY
  :set_NY->NY_Atl NY_Chi NY_Atl NY_Chi;                      ++
          if(jv(msg_dest)=Atl) if(jv(msg_dest)=Chi) .5 .5
  :NY_Atl->sink Atl_Dal;if(jv(msg_dest)=Atl) if(t)
  :NY_Chi->sink Chi_Dal;if(jv(msg_dest)=Chi) if(t)
  :Atlanta->Atl_r_t->set_Atl
  :set_Atl->Atl_Dal Atl_NY Atl_Dal Atl_NY;                   ++
          if(jv(msg_dest)=Dal) if(jv(msg_dest)=NY) .5 .5
  :Atl_Dal->sink Dal_Chi;if(jv(msg_dest)=Dal) if(t)
  :Atl_NY->sink NY_Chi;if(jv(msg_dest)=NY) if(t)
  :Dallas->Dal_r_t->set_Dal
  :set_Dal->Dal_Chi Dal_Atl Dal_Chi Dal_Atl;                 ++
          if(jv(msg_dest)=Chi) if(jv(msg_dest)=Atl) .5 .5
  :Dal_Chi->sink Chi_NY;if(jv(msg_dest)=Chi) if(t)
  :Dal_Atl->sink Atl_NY;if(jv(msg_dest)=Atl) if(t)
  :Chicago->Chi_r_t->set_Chi
  :set_Chi->Chi_NY Chi_Dal Chi_NY Chi_Dal;                   ++
          if(jv(msg_dest)=NY) if(jv(msg_dest)=Dal) .5 .5
  :Chi_NY->sink NY_Atl;if(jv(msg_dest)=NY) if(t)
  :Chi_Dal->sink Dal_Atl;if(jv(msg_dest)=Dal) if(t)
```

The remainder of the dialogue is for definition of simulation specific characteristics. These include the gathering of distributions of performance measures, confidence interval method, initial state definition and stopping criteria. RESQ does not gather distributions of performance measures except where the user specifically requests that a distribution be gathered.

```
QUEUES FOR QUEUEING TIME DIST:resp_time
   VALUES:.2 .4 .6 .8 1 1.2
```

RESQ provides three confidence interval methods, which are described in Section 4.1. In the following we use the regenerative method, with the network initially empty of jobs and with the network empty state being the regeneration state also. The empty state is the default for open chains, so no explicit declaration is needed.

```
CONFIDENCE INTERVAL METHOD:regenerative
REGENERATION STATE DEFINITION -
/*Default initial and regeneration states -- system empty*/
CONFIDENCE LEVEL:90 /*percent*/
```

We choose not to use the automated run length control so that we can demonstrate the interactive simulation capabilities of RESQ. We specify with the guideline that the run will stop at the first occurrence of the regeneration (empty) state after 10,000 response times have completed. However, there is a firm limit of 10 CPU seconds for the simulation run. (These two values may be increased interactively, as we will see.)

```
SEQUENTIAL STOPPING RULE:no
RUN GUIDELINES -
   QUEUES FOR DEPARTURE COUNTS:resp_time
      DEPARTURES:10000
LIMIT - CP SECONDS:10
TRACE:no
END
```

Following is an example of RESQ output for this simulation, using the parameters we suggested before in Chapter 2. The EVAL command initiates simulation. After the EVAL command is given, it issues prompts for the model name and model parameters. The simulation begins and then stops after reaching the 10 second CPU time limit. The results presented exclude results for the last 307 simulated events, the portion of the run since the last occurrence of the system empty state. Simulated events correspond to either arrivals from the sources or completion of service times at the active queues. A regeneration cycle is the period between occurrences of the empty system state. During the first portion of this run the system returned to the empty state 16 times.

```
eval
MODEL:chap4m1
RESQ2 VERSION DATE: MAY 11, 1982 -  TIME: 20:55:49  DATE: 05/21/82
MEAN_LENG:1400
ARRIVL_TIM:0.20 /*used as exponential distribution with this mean*/
RUN END: CPU LIMIT
NO ERRORS DETECTED DURING SIMULATION.    308 DISCARDED EVENTS


                    SIMULATED TIME:      156.65729
                         CPU TIME:           10.64
                 NUMBER OF EVENTS:            7426
                 NUMBER OF CYCLES:              17
```

After the simulation summary, EVAL prompts the users for codes indicating performance measures that are to be displayed.

```
WHAT:/*performance measures?*/ nd(resp_time) /*number departures*/
ELEMENT          NUMBER OF DEPARTURES
RESP_TIME        3167

WHAT:qtbo /*mean queueing time, both points and intervals*/
ELEMENT          MEAN QUEUEING TIME
RESP_TIME        0.41274(0.35023,0.47524)  30.3%
NY_ATL_Q         0.29540(0.25531,0.33549)  27.1%
ATL_DAL_Q        0.28707(0.22609,0.34804)  42.5%
DAL_CHI_Q        0.37318(0.28446,0.46190)  47.5%
CHI_NY_Q         0.40709(0.17755,0.63663) 112.8%
ATL_NY_Q         0.27245(0.25067,0.29424)  16.0%
DAL_ATL_Q        0.27274(0.23592,0.30957)  27.0%
CHI_DAL_Q        0.27577(0.23446,0.31708)  30.0%
NY_CHI_Q         0.26068(0.22197,0.29938)  29.7%

WHAT:
```

The fourth column gives the relative width of the confidence interval in percent, i.e., the width of the confidence interval divided by the point estimate times 100%. After this dialogue is terminated by an empty reply, EVAL gives the user an opportunity to continue the simulation after increasing the guideline and limit previously specified.

```
CONTINUE RUN:yes
GUIDELINE - RTQ DEPARTURES: /*leave this guideline the same*/
LIMIT - CP SECONDS:50
```

Now the run stops after reaching the guideline and continuing for an additional 282 response times, until the system returns to the empty state.

```
RUN END: CPU LIMIT
RUN END: RESP_TIME DEPARTURE GUIDELINE
NO ERRORS DETECTED DURING SIMULATION.

                    SIMULATED TIME:      513.70313
                          CPU TIME:          33.06
                 NUMBER OF EVENTS:          24019
                 NUMBER OF CYCLES:             49

WHAT:nd(resp_time)
ELEMENT          NUMBER OF DEPARTURES
RESP_TIME        10282

WHAT:qtbo
ELEMENT          MEAN QUEUEING TIME
RESP_TIME        0.41095(0.38843,0.43347) 11.0%
NY_ATL_Q         0.34638(0.30003,0.39274) 26.8%
ATL_DAL_Q        0.31668(0.27531,0.35805) 26.1%
DAL_CHI_Q        0.30788(0.27091,0.34486) 24.0%
CHI_NY_Q         0.33074(0.25216,0.40931) 47.5%
ATL_NY_Q         0.29594(0.27046,0.32143) 17.2%
DAL_ATL_Q        0.27924(0.25932,0.29916) 14.3%
CHI_DAL_Q        0.29231(0.26327,0.32136) 19.9%
NY_CHI_Q         0.29129(0.25946,0.32312) 21.9%

WHAT:
```

Again we continue the run. When the new guideline is reached, which is prior to the specified CPU limit, we examine all of the normally provided measures.

```
CONTINUE RUN:yes
GUIDELINE - RESP_TIME DEPARTURES:20000
LIMIT - CP SECONDS:100

RUN END: CPU LIMIT
RUN END: RESP_TIME DEPARTURE GUIDELINE
RUN END: RESP_TIME DEPARTURE GUIDELINE
NO ERRORS DETECTED DURING SIMULATION.

                    SIMULATED TIME:     1014.84351
                          CPU TIME:          64.39
                 NUMBER OF EVENTS:          46928
                 NUMBER OF CYCLES:            100

WHAT:allbo /*all standard measures, both points and intervals*/
ELEMENT          UTILIZATION
RESP_TIME        3.7174E-09(3.5603E-09,3.8746E-09) 0.0%
 NY_R_T          9.6537E-10(9.0408E-10,1.0267E-09) 0.0%
 ATL_R_T         9.2463E-10(8.5699E-10,9.9228E-10) 0.0%
```

```
DAL_R_T         9.1964E-10(8.4642E-10,9.9285E-10)  0.0%
CHI_R_T         9.0779E-10(8.3502E-10,9.8056E-10)  0.0%
NY_ATL_Q        0.51528(0.49314,0.53742)  4.4%
ATL_DAL_Q       0.49960(0.47406,0.52515)  5.1%
DAL_CHI_Q       0.49487(0.47242,0.51731)  4.5%
CHI_NY_Q        0.49359(0.46680,0.52038)  5.4%
ATL_NY_Q        0.50359(0.48061,0.52656)  4.6%
DAL_ATL_Q       0.49477(0.47316,0.51638)  4.3%
CHI_DAL_Q       0.50038(0.47880,0.52196)  4.3%
NY_CHI_Q        0.50183(0.47902,0.52464)  4.6%
```

For a queue with multiple servers or tokens, utilization is determined as the average of all servers or tokens, assuming they are homogeneous. (Tokens are necessarily homogeneous.) For utilization and distribution values, which are constrained to the [0,1] interval, the fourth column gives the absolute width of the confidence interval in percent, i.e., the width of the confidence interval times 100%.

```
ELEMENT         THROUGHPUT
RESP_TIME       19.83359(19.58752,20.07967)  2.5%
 NY_R_T          4.94855(4.81649,5.08060)  5.3%
 ATL_R_T         4.94263(4.81901,5.06626)  5.0%
 DAL_R_T         4.99978(4.87629,5.12328)  4.9%
 CHI_R_T         4.94263(4.80030,5.08497)  5.8%
NY_ATL_Q        3.32071(3.21841,3.42301)  6.2%
ATL_DAL_Q       3.34140(3.22036,3.46245)  7.2%
DAL_CHI_Q       3.30494(3.19591,3.41397)  6.6%
CHI_NY_Q        3.28819(3.16001,3.41637)  7.8%
ATL_NY_Q        3.30691(3.20169,3.41213)  6.4%
DAL_ATL_Q       3.30593(3.20936,3.40250)  5.8%
CHI_DAL_Q       3.29607(3.17221,3.41994)  7.5%
NY_CHI_Q        3.24385(3.14613,3.34157)  6.0%
SET_NY          4.94855
SET_ATL         4.94263
SET_DAL         4.99978
SET_CHI         4.94263
NEW_YORK        4.94855
ATLANTA         4.94263
DALLAS          4.99978
CHICAGO         4.94263
SINK            19.83359

ELEMENT         MEAN QUEUE LENGTH
RESP_TIME       7.98313(7.64571,8.32054)  8.5%
 NY_R_T          2.07312(1.94150,2.20474)  12.7%
 ATL_R_T         1.98563(1.84037,2.13090)  14.6%
 DAL_R_T         1.97490(1.81768,2.13212)  15.9%
 CHI_R_T         1.94947(1.79320,2.10574)  16.0%
NY_ATL_Q        1.05253(0.93344,1.17161)  22.6%
ATL_DAL_Q       1.02826(0.90895,1.14757)  23.2%
```

```
DAL_CHI_Q        1.02396(0.88486,1.16306)  27.2%
CHI_NY_Q         1.00373(0.83123,1.17623)  34.4%
ATL_NY_Q         0.97682(0.88099,1.07265)  19.6%
DAL_ATL_Q        0.93175(0.84269,1.02081)  19.1%
CHI_DAL_Q        0.98241(0.87671,1.08810)  21.5%
NY_CHI_Q         0.98368(0.87805,1.08931)  21.5%


ELEMENT          STANDARD DEVIATION OF QUEUE LENGTH
RESP_TIME        4.19344
  NY_R_T          1.85651
  ATL_R_T         1.84322
  DAL_R_T         1.85416
  CHI_R_T         1.84354
NY_ATL_Q         1.46033
ATL_DAL_Q        1.50998
DAL_CHI_Q        1.56696
CHI_NY_Q         1.54384
ATL_NY_Q         1.33588
DAL_ATL_Q        1.31741
CHI_DAL_Q        1.39669
NY_CHI_Q         1.35321


ELEMENT          MEAN QUEUEING TIME
RESP_TIME        0.40251(0.38803,0.41698)  7.2%
  NY_R_T          0.41894(0.39931,0.43856)  9.4%
  ATL_R_T         0.40174(0.37936,0.42411)  11.1%
  DAL_R_T         0.39500(0.37000,0.42000)  12.7%
  CHI_R_T         0.39442(0.37108,0.41776)  11.8%
NY_ATL_Q         0.31696(0.28660,0.34732)  19.2%
ATL_DAL_Q        0.30773(0.28230,0.33317)  16.5%
DAL_CHI_Q        0.30983(0.27725,0.34241)  21.0%
CHI_NY_Q         0.30525(0.26300,0.34751)  27.7%
ATL_NY_Q         0.29539(0.27360,0.31717)  14.7%
DAL_ATL_Q        0.28184(0.26138,0.30231)  14.5%
CHI_DAL_Q        0.29805(0.27486,0.32125)  15.6%
NY_CHI_Q         0.30325(0.27875,0.32774)  16.2%
```

(These mean queueing times are definitely comparable to those obtained in Section 2.2.1, so the independence assumption does not seem to be a problem for this model.)

```
ELEMENT          STANDARD DEVIATION OF QUEUEING TIME
RESP_TIME        0.40799
  NY_R_T          0.41297
  ATL_R_T         0.40281
  DAL_R_T         0.41459
  CHI_R_T         0.40096
NY_ATL_Q         0.31561
ATL_DAL_Q        0.31359
DAL_CHI_Q        0.33117
CHI_NY_Q         0.33435
```

```
ATL_NY_Q          0.27604
DAL_ATL_Q         0.27134
CHI_DAL_Q         0.28741
NY_CHI_Q          0.28363


ELEMENT           MEAN TOKENS IN USE
RESP_TIME         7.98313(7.64571,8.32054) 8.5%


ELEMENT           MEAN TOTAL TOKENS IN POOL
RESP_TIME         2.1475E+09


ELEMENT           QUEUE LENGTH DISTRIBUTION


ELEMENT           QUEUEING TIME DISTRIBUTION
RESP_TIME         2.00E-01:0.38911(0.38017,0.39805) 1.8%
                  4.00E-01:0.63697(0.62617,0.64777) 2.2%
                  6.00E-01:0.77956(0.76868,0.79044) 2.2%
                  8.00E-01:0.86735(0.85780,0.87690) 1.9%
                  1.00E+00:0.91797(0.91012,0.92583) 1.6%
                  1.20E+00:0.94793(0.94086,0.95501) 1.4%


ELEMENT           DISTRIBUTION OF TOKENS IN USE


ELEMENT           DISTRIBUTION OF TOTAL TOKENS IN POOL


ELEMENT           MAXIMUM QUEUE LENGTH
RESP_TIME         30
  NY_R_T           12
  ATL_R_T          14
  DAL_R_T          17
  CHI_R_T          13
NY_ATL_Q          11
ATL_DAL_Q         14
DAL_CHI_Q         13
CHI_NY_Q          14
ATL_NY_Q          9
DAL_ATL_Q         10
CHI_DAL_Q         11
NY_CHI_Q          10


ELEMENT           MAXIMUM QUEUEING TIME
RESP_TIME         4.11607
```

```
NY_R_T            3.64850
ATL_R_T           3.26095
DAL_R_T           4.11607
CHI_R_T           3.06051
NY_ATL_Q          2.13065
ATL_DAL_Q         2.78842
DAL_CHI_Q         2.27004
CHI_NY_Q          2.62601
ATL_NY_Q          1.74989
DAL_ATL_Q         1.64754
CHI_DAL_Q         1.93313
NY_CHI_Q          2.24017


ELEMENT           OPEN CHAIN POPULATION
C                 7.98313(7.64571,8.32054) 8.5%


ELEMENT           OPEN CHAIN RESPONSE TIME
C                 0.40251(0.38803,0.41698) 7.2%
```

The number of departures is not included in the "all" code, since it can be obtained from the throughput and simulated time.

```
WHAT:nd(resp_time)
ELEMENT           NUMBER OF DEPARTURES
RESP_TIME         20128

WHAT:
```

We choose to stop the simulation at this point. EVAL then gives us the chance to specify new model parameters and run a new simulation.

```
CONTINUE RUN:no

MEAN_LENG:/*opportunity for another run...*/
```


4.3. SUBMODEL DEFINITION

In order to take full advantage of extended queueing network models, one needs a capability for macro definitions of subnetworks. These can be used to develop hierarchical definitions of models in a manner analogous to hierarchical development of programs. Hierarchical models are constructed with the objectives of modularity, clarity, ease of maintenance, etc., which support the overall objective of reducing the effort of developing simulation models.

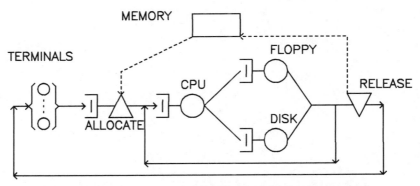

Figure 4.2 - Computer System Model with Memory

In RESQ, the macro definitions of subnetworks are called "submodels." The syntax and structure of submodel definition are essentially the same as in the network definition dialogues we have just described. The main differences are in additional facilities for parameterization, i.e., to provide parameters for connecting submodels to invoking models and other submodels. With a submodel, there is no simulation specific information; this information is provided in the invoking model.

Figure 4.2 shows a computer system model corresponding to the one of Figure 2.9, but with a passive queue added to represent memory contention. Figure 4.3 shows a subnetwork extracted from the network of Figure 4.2, a subnetwork consisting of all of Figure 4.2 except for the terminals. Figure 4.4 depicts a network with invocation of the submodel of Figure 4.3.

Following is a submodel definition corresponding to Figure 4.3. The ordering of major sections is as with RESQ model definitions, as discussed in Section 4.2. First we declare the submodel name, submodel parameters, and constants and variables local to the submodel. Chain parameters are those chains which will be connected to the invoking model or submodel.

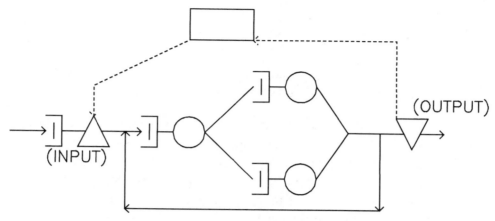

Figure 4.3 - Computer System Submodel

TERMINALS

Figure 4.4 - Network with Submodel Invocation

```
SUBMODEL:cssm /*Computer System SubModel*/
   NUMERIC PARAMETERS:pageframes floppytime disktime cputime
   CHAIN PARAMETERS:chn
   NUMERIC IDENTIFIERS:cpiocycles
      CPIOCYCLES:8
```

Next are queue definitions, as before.

```
QUEUE:floppyq
   TYPE:fcfs
   CLASS LIST:floppy
      SERVICE TIMES:floppytime /* mean of exponential dist. */
QUEUE:diskq
   TYPE:fcfs
   CLASS LIST:disk
      SERVICE TIMES:disktime
QUEUE:cpuq
   TYPE:ps /*processor sharing*/
```

```
        CLASS LIST:cpu
            SERVICE TIMES:cputime
    QUEUE:memory
      TYPE:passive
      TOKENS:pageframes
      DSPL:fcfs
      ALLOCATE NODE LIST:getmemory
          NUMBERS OF TOKENS TO ALLOCATE:discrete(16,.25;32,.5;48,.25)
      RELEASE NODE LIST:freememory
```

The remainder of the submodel definition is for the routing chain. Since it is a chain parameter, to be connected to the invoking model, it has type "external." With external chains one node, the primary entry point to the chain, may be given the synonym "input." Similarly, the primary exit point may be given the synonym "output." (Additional entry and exit points may be defined using "node" parameters.)

```
    CHAIN:chn
        TYPE:external
        INPUT:getmemory
        OUTPUT:freememory
        :getmemory->cpu
        :cpu->floppy disk;.1 .9
        :floppy->freememory cpu;1/cpiocycles 1-1/cpiocycles
        :disk->freememory cpu;1/cpiocycles 1-1/cpiocycles
END OF SUBMODEL CSSM
```

Having defined the submodel, we now define the model corresponding to Figure 4.4.

```
MODEL:csm
    METHOD:simulation
    NUMERIC PARAMETERS:thinktime users pageframes
    NUMERIC IDENTIFIERS:floppytime disktime cputime
        FLOPPYTIME:.22
        DISKTIME:.019
        CPUTIME:.05
    NUMERIC IDENTIFIERS:cpiocycles
        CPIOCYCLES:8
    QUEUE:terminalsq
        TYPE:is /*infinite server*/
        CLASS LIST:terminals
            SERVICE TIMES:thinktime
```

After the queue definitions (and other elements in the network proper, e.g., set nodes) come submodel definitions and invocations. This definition assumes that the submodel definition has been stored in a library. Since each submodel may be invoked repeatedly, each invocation is named.

```
INCLUDE:cssm /*submodel definition*/
INVOCATION:host
   TYPE:cssm
   PAGEFRAMES:pageframes
   FLOPPYTIME:floppytime
   DISKTIME:disktime
   CPUTIME:cputime
   CHN:interactiv
```

The chain of the model proper is now defined, using the synonyms for the allocate and release nodes,

```
CHAIN:interactiv
   TYPE:closed
   POPULATION:users
   :terminals->host.input
   :host.output->terminals
```

and simulation specific information is provided. This definition will use the regenerative method with the regeneration state of all users at the terminals. The automated stopping rule will run the simulation until the confidence interval for the mean queueing time for the memory queue (the mean response time seen by the users) has relative width no greater than 10%.

```
QUEUES FOR QUEUEING TIME DIST:host.memory
   VALUES:1 2 3 4 5 6 7 8
QUEUES FOR QUEUE LENGTH DIST:host.memory
   MAX VALUE:users/2
CONFIDENCE INTERVAL METHOD:regenerative
REGENERATION STATE DEFINITION-
CHAIN:interactiv
   NODE LIST:terminals
   REGEN POP:users
   INIT POP:users
CONFIDENCE LEVEL:90
SEQUENTIAL STOPPING RULE:yes
   QUEUES TO BE CHECKED:host.memory
      MEASURES:qt
      ALLOWED WIDTHS:10
SAMPLING PERIOD GUIDELINES-
   QUEUES FOR DEPARTURE COUNTS:host.memory
      DEPARTURES:1000
LIMIT - CP SECONDS:300
TRACE:no
END
```

4.4. FURTHER READING

More detailed descriptions of the current version of RESQ are given by Sauer, MacNair and Kurose [23,24,25,26]. A number of other references in the Bibliography describe previous versions of RESQ. Simulation tools related to RESQ include the Queueing Network Analysis Package (QNAP) [13] and the Performance Analyst's Workbench System (PAWS) [4].

Chapter 7 of Sauer and Chandy [19] includes Pascal programs for an extended queueing network simulation system and exercises suggesting further development of those programs. Those programs as given include basic passive queues and fission and fusion nodes. As given they are sufficient for simulating some of the networks we use as examples. By performing the appropriate exercises, e.g., by adding job variables, create and destroy nodes and priority scheduling, the reader would have a simulation system capable of simulating all of our examples. However, the system as given by Sauer and Chandy does not have the user interface capabilities of RESQ, i.e., the networks to be simulated are defined by writing a Pascal program which calls the simulation system.

Statistical analysis of simulation output is discussed in Chapter 7 of Sauer and Chandy [19]. A more comprehensive discussion of simulation output analysis is given by Welch [34].

CHAPTER 5

PROTOCOL REPRESENTATIONS

We are now ready to begin our examples in earnest, now that we have defined extended queueing networks and presented the syntax used in our formal definitions. In this chapter we will consider addition of several basic protocol mechanisms to the network model of Figure 4.1 and the RESQ realization of that model given in the last chapter. Before we do this, we will first make the model more modular, adding a submodel to represent a city and invoking this submodel for each of the four cities.

The mechanisms we wish to consider here are acknowledgements, time outs, packetizing of messages, simple adaptive routing decisions and simple flow control mechanisms. We will treat these individually but generally not in combinations. We leave for the reader a general exercise of fitting together combinations of the mechanism representations we describe. We will also intersperse a few specific exercises for refinement of the represent-ations and/or variations on the examples.

5.1. MODULAR REPRESENTATIONS

Figure 4.1 and the corresponding RESQ representation, though perhaps adequate if considered as a final objective, are unsuitable for the develop-ment we desire. The characteristics we wish to represent will usually be duplicated for each city, so to work directly with that figure and RESQ dialogue would mean corresponding duplications in the model. Adding cities to the network would be a tedious process, at best.

Since the cities are the foci of our system, the model should have a modular representation of a generic city, e.g., a RESQ submodel, and repeated instances of the generic city with parameters appropriate to the individual cities. Figure 5.1 suggests the top level network representation with this modularization, and Figure 5.2 details the city module.

75

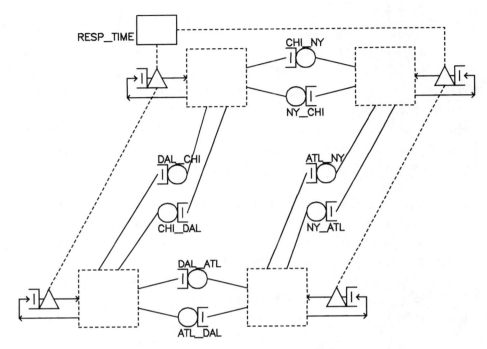

Figure 5.1 - Cities Represented by Submodels

Together these two figures are equivalent to the network of Figure 4.1. There is one minor difference, the "dummy" node, "decide" in the submodel of Figure 5.2. A dummy node is the extended queueing network equivalent of a "no op" machine instruction, i.e., it has no effect. Dummy nodes are not strictly necessary, but are often useful in network descriptions. In this case the dummy node "decide" is being introduced in anticipation of its usage in routing descriptions in following sections.

There is a more substantial difference between the submodel of Figure 5.2 and the submodel of Figure 4.4. In Figure 4.4 there was a single entry point and a single exit point for the submodel. This is not the case in Figure 5.2. In this subnetwork there are two primary entry points, for traffic coming from the network in clockwise and counterclockwise directions, and two primary exits, one for each direction. In addition there are a secondary exit and a secondary entrance for jobs to visit an allocate node of

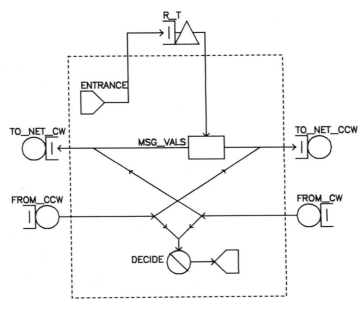

Figure 5.2 - City Submodel

the response time queue. Though we have not explicitly stated this before, our concept of subnetworks assumes that queues do not cross subnetwork boundaries, i.e., a queue is entirely within a subnetwork or entirely outside of a subnetwork. In this case we wish to have a single passive queue measuring all response times, so the passive queue must be outside the subnetwork and there must be a means for jobs to leave the subnetwork temporarily to acquire a token from the passive queue.

In RESQ we use the "node parameters" mentioned in Section 4.3 to declare nodes that are outside of a submodel which we wish to include in the submodel routing. In the submodel of Figure 5.2 there are five node parameters, the allocate node and the four links. For example, in the invocation of the submodel for Dallas, the allocate node parameter "r__t" will have as its value the "Dal__r__t" allocate node, the "to__net__ccw" node parameter will have as its value the class "Dal__Atl," the "from__cw" node parameter will have as its value the class "Atl__Dal," the "from__ccw" node parameter will have as its value the class "Chi__Dal" and the "to__net__cw" node parameter will have as its value the class "Dal__Chi."

Following is a RESQ submodel definition corresponding to Figure 5.2:

```
SUBMODEL:city
   NUMERIC PARAMETERS:city_code
   NUMERIC PARAMETERS:cw_city /*clockwise city code*/
   NUMERIC PARAMETERS:ccw_city /*counterclockwise*/
   NODE PARAMETERS:r_t
   NODE PARAMETERS:to_net_cw to_net_ccw
   NODE PARAMETERS:from_cw from_ccw
   CHAIN PARAMETERS:c
   SET NODES:msg_vals
   ASSIGNMENT LIST:jv(msg_dest)=dest_dist(city_code)   ++
                   jv(msg_leng)=msg_l_dist             ++
                   jv(msg_origin)=city_code            ++
                   jv(msg_type)=data
   DUMMY NODES:decide
   CHAIN:c
      TYPE:external
      SOURCE LIST:entrance
      ARRIVAL TIMES:arrivl_tim
      /*Traffic for network: */
      :entrance->r_t->msg_vals
      :msg_vals->to_net_cw to_net_ccw to_net_cw to_net_ccw;  ++
       if(jv(msg_dest)=cw_city) if(jv(msg_dest)=ccw_city) .5 .5
      /*Traffic from network: */
      :from_cw->decide to_net_cw;if(jv(msg_dest)=city_code) if(t)
      :from_ccw->decide to_net_ccw;if(jv(msg_dest)=city_code) if(t)
      :decide->sink
END OF SUBMODEL CITY
```

The distribution identifier "dest__dist" is assumed to be defined in the invoking submodel, as are the new numeric identifiers "msg__origin" and "msg__type" which we will use in our developments in the following sections. Note especially that the chain definition in the submodel encompasses the entire routing definition from the previous model of Section 4 — the chain definition in the invoking model will be empty of routing statements.

Following is a model definition with four invocations of submodel "city." This definition has a few additions in anticipation of the developments coming up, but is essentially the same model as that of Chapter 4 except for the use of submodels. The additions are definitions of additional job variables and the definition of the link queues as non-preemptive priority queues. The priorities are given by a job variable. This variable will have the same value (2) for all jobs with the above definition of submodel "city," so the link queues will actually have FCFS scheduling, as before. The model uses the sequential stopping procedure to determine run length, but otherwise will produce the same simulation results as before except for the statistical variability of simulation.

```
MODEL:chap5m1
   METHOD:simulation
   NUMERIC PARAMETERS:mean_leng /*mean message length*/
   DISTRIBUTION PARAMETERS:arrivl_tim /*arrival_times*/
   NUMERIC IDENTIFIERS:NY Atl Dal Chi
      NY:1
      ATL:2
      DAL:3
      CHI:4
   NUMERIC IDENTIFIERS:msg_dest msg_leng msg_origin msg_type
      MSG_DEST:0    /*JV(0) to be used to store destination    */
      MSG_LENG:1    /*JV(1) to be used to store length         */
      MSG_ORIGIN:2  /*JV(2) to be used to store origin         */
      MSG_TYPE:3    /*JV(3) to be used to store type (data or ack) */
   NUMERIC IDENTIFIERS:ack data
      ACK:1
      DATA:2
   DISTRIBUTION IDENTIFIERS:msg_l_dist /*message length */
      MSG_L_DIST:standard(mean_leng,1) /*exponential     */
   DISTRIBUTION IDENTIFIERS:dest_dist(4)
      /*Destination for messages leaving a city*/
      DEST_DIST: /*NY */ discrete(Atl,1/3;Dal,1/3;Chi,1/3) ++
                 /*Atl*/ discrete(NY ,1/3;Dal,1/3;Chi,1/3) ++
                 /*Dal*/ discrete(NY ,1/3;Atl,1/3;Chi,1/3) ++
                 /*Chi*/ discrete(NY ,1/3;Dal,1/3;Atl,1/3)
   MAX JV:3 /*maximum subscript*/
   QUEUE TYPE:basic_link
      NUMERIC PARAMETERS:prop_delay
      NODE PARAMETERS:class_name
      TYPE:prty /*non-preemptive priority*/
      CLASS LIST:class_name
         SERVICE TIMES:standard(jv(msg_leng)/9600+prop_delay,0)
         PRIORITIES:jv(msg_type)
   END OF QUEUE TYPE BASIC_LINK
   QUEUE:NY_Atl_q
      TYPE:basic_link
      PROP_DELAY:.00408    /*invocation with matching */
      CLASS_NAME:NY_Atl    /*     of names and values */
   QUEUE:Atl_Dal_q
      TYPE:basic_link: .00377; Atl_Dal /*positional invocation*/
```

```
QUEUE:Dal_Chi_q
   TYPE:basic_link: .00423; Dal_Chi
QUEUE:Chi_NY_q
   TYPE:basic_link: .00377; Chi_NY
QUEUE:Atl_NY_q
   TYPE:basic_link: .00408; Atl_NY
QUEUE:Dal_Atl_q
   TYPE:basic_link: .00377; Dal_Atl
QUEUE:Chi_Dal_q
   TYPE:basic_link: .00423; Chi_Dal
QUEUE:NY_Chi_q
   TYPE:basic_link: .00377; NY_Chi
QUEUE:resp_time
   TYPE:passive
   TOKENS:2147483647   /* "infinity" -- 2**31-1 */
   DSPL:fcfs
   ALLOCATE NODE LIST:NY_r_t Atl_r_t Dal_r_t Chi_r_t
      NUMBERS OF TOKENS TO ALLOCATE:1
INCLUDE:city /*submodel definition stored in library*/
INVOCATION:New_York
   TYPE:city
   CITY_CODE:NY
   CW_CITY:Atl
   CCW_CITY:Chi
   R_T:NY_r_t
   TO_NET_CW:NY_Atl
   TO_NET_CCW:NY_Chi
   FROM_CW:Chi_NY
   FROM_CCW:Atl_NY
   C:c
INVOCATION:Atlanta
   TYPE:city:Atl;Dal;NY;Atl_r_t;Atl_Dal;Atl_NY;NY_Atl;Dal_Atl;c
INVOCATION:Dallas
   TYPE:city:Dal;Chi;Atl;Dal_r_t;Dal_Chi;Dal_Atl;Atl_Dal;Chi_Dal;c
INVOCATION:Chicago
   TYPE:city:Chi;NY;Dal;Chi_r_t;Chi_NY;Chi_Dal;Dal_Chi;NY_Chi;c
CHAIN:c
   TYPE:open
QUEUES FOR QUEUEING TIME DIST:resp_time
   VALUES:.2 .4 .6 .8 1 1.2
CONFIDENCE INTERVAL METHOD:regenerative
/*Initial & regeneration states are the same, with system empty:*/
REGENERATION STATE DEFINITION -
CONFIDENCE LEVEL:90
SEQUENTIAL STOPPING RULE:yes
   QUEUES TO BE CHECKED:resp_time
      MEASURES:qt
      ALLOWED WIDTHS:5
SAMPLING PERIOD GUIDELINES -
   QUEUES FOR DEPARTURE COUNTS:resp_time
      DEPARTURES:20000
LIMIT - CP SECONDS:1000
TRACE:no
```

5.2. ACKNOWLEDGEMENTS

Messages may be lost in communication networks because of uncorrectable transmission errors, buffer overflow or other problems. Usually a sender of a message will expect an acknowledgement from the recipient indicating the message was satisfactorily received. We considered this to a limited extent in Section 2.1.3.2 in discussing queues in isolation. However, consideration of acknowledgements in a numerically solved queueing network is problematic because of the violations of product form assumptions, i.e., the radically different message size distributions (acknowledgements are typically short and of fixed length).

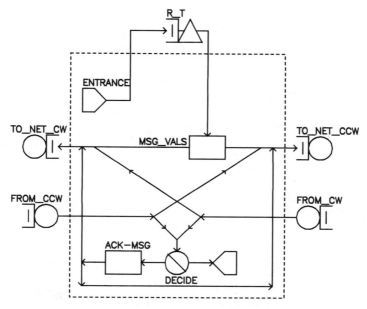

Figure 5.3 - City Submodel with Acknowledgements

In this section we wish to consider simple end to end acknowledgements. Effectively what the model says is that once a job (representing a message) reaches its destination, the job will have its length set to that of an acknowledgement, say 32 bits, and the job will turn around and go back to its origin. Figure 5.3 illustrates the modifications to the subnetwork of Figure 5.2 for this purpose. When a job reaches the dummy node "decide," the routing decision will be made based on a job variable indicating whether the job represents a data message or an acknowledgement. If the job represents a data message, it goes from "decide" to the set node "ack__msg." At "ack__msg" the job variable representing the destination is set to the message origin, the job variable representing the message length is set to 32 and the job variable representing message type is set to indicate an acknowledgement. If the job represents an acknowledgement, it goes to the sink and the response time token is released.

Following is the modified version of submodel "city."

```
SUBMODEL:city
   NUMERIC PARAMETERS:city_code
   NUMERIC PARAMETERS:cw_city /*clockwise city code*/
   NUMERIC PARAMETERS:ccw_city /*counterclockwise*/
   NODE PARAMETERS:r_t
   NODE PARAMETERS:to_net_cw to_net_ccw
   NODE PARAMETERS:from_cw from_ccw
   CHAIN PARAMETERS:c
   SET NODES:msg_vals
   ASSIGNMENT LIST:jv(msg_dest)=dest_dist(city_code)    ++
                  jv(msg_leng)=msg_l_dist               ++
                  jv(msg_origin)=city_code              ++
                  jv(msg_type)=data
   SET NODES:ack_msg
   ASSIGNMENT LIST:jv(msg_dest)=jv(msg_origin)          ++
                  jv(msg_leng)=32                       ++
                  jv(msg_type)=ack
   DUMMY NODES:decide
   CHAIN:c
      TYPE:external
      SOURCE LIST:entrance
      ARRIVAL TIMES:arrivl_tim
      /*Traffic for network: */
      :entrance->r_t->msg_vals
      :msg_vals->to_net_cw to_net_ccw to_net_cw to_net_ccw;  ++
       if(jv(msg_dest)=cw_city) if(jv(msg_dest)=ccw_city) .5 .5
      /*Traffic from network: */
      :from_cw->decide to_net_cw;if(jv(msg_dest)=city_code) if(t)
      :from_ccw->decide to_net_ccw;if(jv(msg_dest)=city_code) if(t)
```

```
    :decide->sink ack_msg;if(jv(msg_type)=ack) if(t)
    :ack_msg->to_net_cw to_net_ccw to_net_cw to_net_ccw;  ++
     if(jv(msg_dest)=cw_city) if(jv(msg_dest)=ccw_city) .5 .5
END OF SUBMODEL CITY
```

The definition of the invoking model may be exactly the same as in the previous section. Note that in that definition we used a non-preemptive priority queue type for the link queues. Those queues will give priority to acknowledgements over data messages. (Recall the discussion in Section 2.1.3.2.) We might obtain the following results from RESQ:

```
MODEL:chap5m1
RESQ2 VERSION DATE: MAY 11, 1982 - TIME: 00:13:57 DATE: 05/25/82
MEAN_LENG:1400
ARRIVL_TIM:0.20 /*used as exponential distribution with this mean*/
SAMPLING PERIOD END: RESP_TIME DEPARTURE GUIDELINE
SAMPLING PERIOD END: RESP_TIME DEPARTURE GUIDELINE
NO ERRORS DETECTED DURING SIMULATION.

            SIMULATED TIME:     2033.21240
                 CPU TIME:          280.17
        NUMBER OF EVENTS:          148756
        NUMBER OF CYCLES:             150

WHAT:nd(resp_time)
INVOCATION      ELEMENT        NUMBER OF DEPARTURES
                RESP_TIME      40518
```

As we would expect, there is a slight increase in link utilizations due to the acknowledgement traffic.

```
WHAT:utbo
INVOCATION      ELEMENT        UTILIZATION
                RESP_TIME      4.8890E-09(4.7486E-09,5.0293E-09) 0.0%
                NY_ATL_Q       0.52656(0.51139,0.54173) 3.0%
                ATL_DAL_Q      0.51921(0.50380,0.53461) 3.1%
                DAL_CHI_Q      0.52918(0.51217,0.54620) 3.4%
                CHI_NY_Q       0.52663(0.50979,0.54346) 3.4%
                ATL_NY_Q       0.51970(0.50496,0.53443) 2.9%
                DAL_ATL_Q      0.51413(0.49767,0.53059) 3.3%
                CHI_DAL_Q      0.52317(0.50695,0.53938) 3.2%
                NY_CHI_Q       0.53111(0.51714,0.54508) 2.8%
```

The mean response time increases by roughly 120 ms., but this is a more realistic response time measure, because the sender really is getting a response.

```
WHAT:qtbo(*)
INVOCATION        ELEMENT          MEAN QUEUEING TIME
                  RESP_TIME        0.52684(0.51431,0.53937)  4.8%
                   NY_R_T           0.52695(0.51324,0.54067)  5.2%
                  ATL_R_T           0.52185(0.50729,0.53642)  5.6%
                  DAL_R_T           0.52004(0.50353,0.53654)  6.3%
                  CHI_R_T           0.53850(0.51654,0.56046)  8.2%
                  NY_ATL_Q         0.19697(0.18780,0.20614)  9.3%
                  ATL_DAL_Q        0.19571(0.18324,0.20819) 12.7%
                  DAL_CHI_Q        0.20395(0.19309,0.21481) 10.6%
                  CHI_NY_Q         0.21121(0.18972,0.23269) 20.3%
                  ATL_NY_Q         0.19026(0.18117,0.19934)  9.5%
                  DAL_ATL_Q        0.18368(0.17552,0.19184)  8.9%
                  CHI_DAL_Q        0.19846(0.18441,0.21251) 14.2%
                  NY_CHI_Q         0.19732(0.18769,0.20694)  9.8%


WHAT:qtdbo
INVOCATION        ELEMENT          QUEUEING TIME DISTRIBUTION
                  RESP_TIME        2.00E-01:0.25315(0.24681,0.25948)  1.3%
                                   4.00E-01:0.49993(0.49086,0.50899)  1.8%
                                   6.00E-01:0.67567(0.66662,0.68473)  1.8%
                                   8.00E-01:0.79078(0.78277,0.79880)  1.6%
                                   1.00E+00:0.86636(0.85960,0.87311)  1.4%
                                   1.20E+00:0.91621(0.91103,0.92139)  1.0%

WHAT:
CONTINUE RUN:no
MEAN_LENG:
```

The primary limitations of this model of acknowledgements are that we are not considering the lost messages or negative acknowledgements for erroneously transmitted messages. We will now consider lost messages and suggest exercises relating to negative acknowledgements.

5.3. TIME OUTS

When a computer transmits a message to another computer over a potentially unreliable medium, it will normally retain a copy of that message for retransmission in case of failure of the initial transmission. The retransmission will typically be triggered by one of two events: either an explicit negative acknowledgement will be received, asking that the message be resent, or some arbitrarily determined time will elapse. In this latter, "time out," case, the initial transmission is presumed lost (though in fact it may just have been excessively delayed).

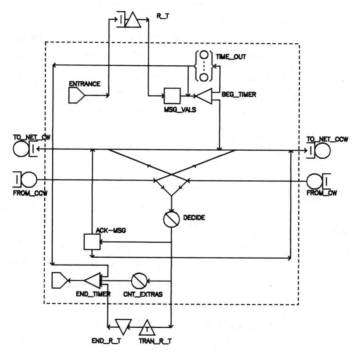

Figure 5.4 - City Submodel with Time Outs

Figure 5.4 depicts an approach to representation of these time outs in our "city" submodel. It is based on fission nodes, fusion nodes and the transfer of tokens from parent to child. The representation assumes status functions are available to determine how many tokens a job holds of a particular passive queue and to determine how many relatives a job has at particular locations. Other representations of time__outs, for example, using split nodes and global variables, are also possible.

The normal sequence of events for a message is as follows. (1) After the job representing the message has obtained its response time token and has had its characteristics set at set node "msg__vals," it proceeds to the fission node "beg__timer." (2) The parent (original) job leaving "beg__timer" goes to an infinite server queue for a delay representing the time out, at class "time__out." (3) The child leaving "beg__timer" proceeds through the network as in our last example, being turned around as an acknowledgement and ending up at dummy node "decide" in the city of origin. (4) The child leaving "decide" determines that it has only one relative (its parent) and that relative is at class "time__out." (5) The child goes to transfer node "tran__r__t" and obtains the response time token held by its parent. (6) The child releases the response time token (thus ending the measured response time) and goes to fusion node "end__timer." (7) Some time later, the parent completes its service time at class "time__out" and determines that it no longer holds its response time token. (8) The parent goes to fusion node "end__timer," the child is destroyed and the parent goes to the sink.

If the child does not return to the origin before the end of the time out, then the following events occur. (1) The parent will determine that it still has its response time token. (2) The parent goes to fission node "beg__timer" again, creating another child, which traverses the network similarly to the first child. (3) The first of the children to arrive at dummy node "decide" in its city of origin will determine that it has no relatives at the fusion node "end__timer," and will follow the path through the transfer and release nodes to the fusion node as in the normal case. (4) When the remaining children (the time out may happen several times for the same message) arrive at "decide" in their city of origin, they will determine that they already have a relative at fusion node "end__timer" and will go directly to "end__timer" without attempting to obtain the response time token (which their parent no longer possesses). (Actually they do not go quite directly, but rather through dummy node "cnt__extras" which we use to count the number of extra children taking this path.) (5) Eventually all of the children and the parent will have arrived at the fusion node "end__timer" and the parent will proceed to the sink.

Following is a RESQ definition of this new version of submodel "city."

```
SUBMODEL:city
   NUMERIC PARAMETERS:city_code
   NUMERIC PARAMETERS:cw_city /*clockwise city code*/
   NUMERIC PARAMETERS:ccw_city /*counterclockwise*/
   NODE PARAMETERS:r_t tran_r_t end_r_t
   NODE PARAMETERS:to_net_cw to_net_ccw
   NODE PARAMETERS:from_cw from_ccw
   CHAIN PARAMETERS:c
   QUEUE:time_out_q
      TYPE:is
      CLASS LIST:time_out
         SERVICE TIMES:standard(3,0)
   SET NODES:msg_vals
   ASSIGNMENT LIST:jv(msg_dest)=dest_dist(city_code)   ++
                   jv(msg_leng)=msg_l_dist              ++
                   jv(msg_origin)=city_code             ++
                   jv(msg_type)=data
   SET NODES:ack_msg
   ASSIGNMENT LIST:jv(msg_dest)=jv(msg_origin)          ++
                   jv(msg_leng)=32                      ++
                   jv(msg_type)=ack
   FISSION NODES:beg_timer
   FUSION NODES:end_timer
   DUMMY NODES:decide to_ntwrk cnt_extras
   CHAIN:c
      TYPE:external
      SOURCE LIST:entrance
      ARRIVAL TIMES:arrivl_tim
      /*Traffic for network: */
      :entrance->r_t->msg_vals->beg_timer
      :beg_timer->time_out to_ntwrk;fission
      :to_ntwrk->to_net_cw to_net_ccw to_net_cw to_net_ccw;  ++
       if(jv(msg_dest)=cw_city) if(jv(msg_dest)=ccw_city) .5 .5
      :time_out->end_timer beg_timer;if(th(resp_time)=0) if(t)
      /*Traffic from network: */
      :from_cw->decide to_net_cw;if(jv(msg_dest)=city_code) if(t)
      :from_ccw->decide to_net_ccw;if(jv(msg_dest)=city_code) if(t)
      :decide->ack_msg;if(jv(msg_type)=data)
      :ack_msg->to_net_cw to_net_ccw to_net_cw to_net_ccw;  ++
       if(jv(msg_dest)=cw_city) if(jv(msg_dest)=ccw_city) .5 .5
      :decide->tran_r_t;if(rj(time_out)=rj or rj(end_timer)=0)
      :tran_r_t->end_r_t->end_timer
      :decide->cnt_extras->end_timer
      :end_timer->sink
END OF SUBMODEL CITY
```

We have assumed the timer interval is three seconds. The status function "th(<queue name>)" returns the number of tokens (if any) a job holds at the specified passive queue. The status function "rj(<node name>)" returns the number of related jobs (if any) at the specified node. The status function "rj" (without argument) returns the number of related jobs (if any) in the entire network. In the routing from "decide" to "tran__r__t," the first alternative of the predicate is equivalent to "rj=1 and rj(time__out)=1" for the purposes of this model since rj(time__out) is always zero or one.

The following changes are needed in the invoking model. First, the transfer and release nodes must be declared for the response time queue.

```
QUEUE:resp_time
   TYPE:passive
   TOKENS:2147483647    /* "infinity" -- 2**31-1 */
   DSPL:fcfs
   ALLOCATE NODE LIST:NY_r_t Atl_r_t Dal_r_t Chi_r_t
      NUMBERS OF TOKENS TO ALLOCATE:1
   TRANSFER NODE LIST:NY_tr_rt Atl_tr_rt Dal_tr_rt Chi_tr_rt
      NUMBERS OF TOKENS TO TRANSFER:1
   RELEASE NODE LIST:NY_end_rt Atl_end_rt Dal_end_rt Chi_end_rt
```

(A negative number of tokens to transfer would indicate transfer from child to parent.) Second, these new nodes must be included in the invocations, e.g.,

```
INVOCATION:New_York
   TYPE:city
   CITY_CODE:NY
   CW_CITY:Atl
   CCW_CITY:Chi
   R_T:NY_r_t
   TRAN_R_T:NY_tr_rt
   END_R_T:NY_end_rt
   TO_NET_CW:NY_Atl
   TO_NET_CCW:NY_Chi
   FROM_CW:Chi_NY
   FROM_CCW:Atl_NY
   C:c
```

Third, we cannot use the regenerative method for confidence intervals because of the jobs at the time out queues, so we choose to use the spectral method.

```
CONFIDENCE INTERVAL METHOD:spectral
INITIAL STATE DEFINITION -
CONFIDENCE LEVEL:90
SEQUENTIAL STOPPING RULE:yes
  CONFIDENCE INTERVAL QUEUES:resp_time resp_time
    MEASURES:               qt         qtd
```

```
         ALLOWED WIDTHS:                5          5
          CONFIDENCE INTERVAL QUEUES:NY_Atl_q Atl_Dal_q Dal_Chi_q Chi_NY_q
             MEASURES:                 qt         qt         qt         qt
             ALLOWED WIDTHS:          200        200        200        200
          CONFIDENCE INTERVAL QUEUES:NY_Chi_q Chi_Dal_q Dal_Atl_q Atl_NY_q
             MEASURES:                 qt         qt         qt         qt
             ALLOWED WIDTHS:          200        200        200        200
       INITIAL PORTION DISCARDED:5 /*percent of initial sampling period*/
       INITIAL PERIOD LIMITS-
          QUEUES FOR DEPARTURE COUNTS:resp_time
             DEPARTURES:20000
       LIMIT - CP SECONDS:1500
       TRACE:no
END
```

Using these definitions we might get the following results from RESQ.

```
MODEL:chap5m2
RESQ2 VERSION DATE: MAY 11, 1982 - TIME: 17:07:50 DATE: 05/25/82
MEAN_LENG:1400
ARRIVL_TIM:0.20 /*used as exponential distribution with this mean*/
SAMPLING PERIOD END: RESP_TIME DEPARTURE LIMIT
SAMPLING PERIOD END: RESP_TIME DEPARTURE LIMIT
SAMPLING PERIOD END: RESP_TIME DEPARTURE LIMIT
SAMPLING PERIOD END: RESP_TIME DEPARTURE LIMIT
```

The discarded events in the following message are those for the first 1000 ($.05 \times 20,000$) response times.

```
NO ERRORS DETECTED DURING SIMULATION.   4644 DISCARDED EVENTS

                 SIMULATED TIME:     3219.21509
                      CPU TIME:         655.03
               NUMBER OF EVENTS:        299990
```

Messages will only be retransmitted in this model when messages have unusually large delays. Thus there are few retransmissions.

```
WHAT:nd(resp_time,New_York.cnt_extras,Atlanta.cnt_extras, ++
            Dallas.cnt_extras,Chicago.cnt_extras)
INVOCATION       ELEMENT        NUMBER OF DEPARTURES
                 RESP_TIME       64125
NEW_YORK         CNT_EXTRAS      15
ATLANTA          CNT_EXTRAS      20
DALLAS           CNT_EXTRAS      23
CHICAGO          CNT_EXTRAS      12
```

```
WHAT:lng(resp_time,New_York.time_out_q,Atlanta.time_out_q, ++
            Dallas.time_out_q,Chicago.time_out_q)
```

INVOCATION	ELEMENT	FINAL LENGTHS
	RESP_TIME	8
NEW_YORK	TIME_OUT_Q	17
ATLANTA	TIME_OUT_Q	18
DALLAS	TIME_OUT_Q	13
CHICAGO	TIME_OUT_Q	18

The utilizations and queueing times are essentially the same as before.

```
WHAT:ut
```

INVOCATION	ELEMENT	UTILIZATION
	RESP_TIME	4.8783E-09
	NY_ATL_Q	0.52107
	ATL_DAL_Q	0.51175
	DAL_CHI_Q	0.52365
	CHI_NY_Q	0.53115
	ATL_NY_Q	0.51786
	DAL_ATL_Q	0.51341
	CHI_DAL_Q	0.53404
	NY_CHI_Q	0.53684
NEW_YORK	TIME_OUT_Q	0.00000
ATLANTA	TIME_OUT_Q	0.00000
DALLAS	TIME_OUT_Q	0.00000
CHICAGO	TIME_OUT_Q	0.00000

```
WHAT:qtbo
```

INVOCATION	ELEMENT	MEAN QUEUEING TIME	
	RESP_TIME	0.52582(0.51401,0.53763)	4.5%
	NY_ATL_Q	0.19532(0.18598,0.20466)	9.6%
	ATL_DAL_Q	0.18893(0.17921,0.19864)	10.3%
	DAL_CHI_Q	0.20060(0.18586,0.21533)	14.7%
	CHI_NY_Q	0.20013(0.18989,0.21036)	10.2%
	ATL_NY_Q	0.19274(0.18329,0.20219)	9.8%
	DAL_ATL_Q	0.18947(0.17872,0.20021)	11.3%
	CHI_DAL_Q	0.20629(0.19158,0.22101)	14.3%
	NY_CHI_Q	0.20379(0.19426,0.21332)	9.4%
NEW_YORK	TIME_OUT_Q	3.00000	
ATLANTA	TIME_OUT_Q	3.00000	
DALLAS	TIME_OUT_Q	3.00000	
CHICAGO	TIME_OUT_Q	3.00000	

```
WHAT:qtdbo
```

INVOCATION	ELEMENT	QUEUEING TIME DISTRIBUTION	
	RESP_TIME	2.00E-01:0.25603(0.25081,0.26125)	1.0%
		4.00E-01:0.50002(0.49115,0.50890)	1.8%
		6.00E-01:0.67247(0.66392,0.68102)	1.7%
		8.00E-01:0.78894(0.78149,0.79639)	1.5%
		1.00E+00:0.86520(0.85919,0.87121)	1.2%
		1.20E+00:0.91529(0.90863,0.92195)	1.3%

```
WHAT:
```

```
CONTINUE RUN:no
MEAN_LENG:
```

Exercise 5.1 - Negative Acknowledgements without Time Outs. The models given so far do not consider explicit negative acknowledgements (which occur because of uncorrected transmission errors). Develop a version of the city subnetwork which includes negative acknowledgements. In this exercise do not incorporate time outs for lost or excessively delayed messages.

Exercise 5.2 - Negative Acknowledgements and Time Outs. Combine the time outs of the last example and the negative acknowledgements of Exercise 5.1 in a single version of the city subnetwork.

Exercise 5.3 - Store and Forward Buffering. Most of our discussion and examples so far have assumed that the computers involved had sufficient buffers for messages that we could ignore contention for buffers. In practice, buffer contention may be sufficient to cause loss of messages and other problems. It is a straightforward application of passive queues to represent buffer contention. A token of the passive queue represents a unit of buffer space. One or more tokens are allocated when buffer space is required and are released when the space is no longer needed. The "ta(<queue_name>)" status function provides the current number of tokens available at the specified queue. A job requiring buffers can use this function to determine whether sufficient buffers are available or whether it should "get lost."

Often communication networks will operate in a store and forward manner, where intermediate nodes buffer messages and acknowledge receipt of messages so that the sending node or previous intermediate nodes may free the buffers held by these messages. (An example of an intermediate communication network node in our hypothetical four city network would be Atlanta for a

message going from Dallas to New York by way of Atlanta.) Extend the city subnetwork to consider store and
forward buffering with acknowledgements.

Exercise 5.4 - Congestion Control. In a store and forward
system, a network node may wish to conserve buffers if
and when its buffer supply is depleted. For example, a
node might tell its neighbors not to transmit data to it
when its buffer occupancy level reaches 75% and then
tell its neighbors to resume normal operation when buffer occupancy drops back below 50%. Construct an
extended queueing network representation for such a
mechanism. A sketch of such a representation is given by
Sauer [17]. (You may wish to consider deadlock preven-
tion in your representation.)

5.4. PACKETIZED MESSAGES

A potentially severe problem with non-preemptive scheduling is that a
long service time for one job can cause excessive delay for many other jobs
with short service times. For this reason processors are usually scheduled
using a preemptive resume mechanism where sufficient information about
processor state is retained to allow resumption of processing at the point of
suspension. With resources such as disks and communication links this is
less practical. However, essentially the same effect can be obtained with
communication links by dividing messages into packets no larger than some
size chosen to avoid monopolization of a link by a single packet.

Fission and fusion nodes are naturally used to represent division of a
message into several packets and the reassembly of these packets into
messages. Figure 5.5 depicts addition of fission and fusion nodes for this
purpose to the city subnetwork of Figure 5.3. If a message is longer than a
single packet, it goes to the fission node "separate" one or more times to
generate children representing packets. The job variable giving the message
length of the parent is decremented by the amount of data that may be
included in a packet and the job variable of the child giving the message
length is set to the packet size (which includes data, control information and

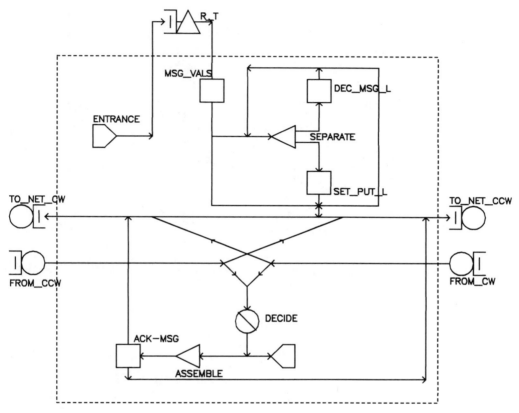

Figure 5.5 - City Submodel with Packetized Messages

error correction information). The packets traverse the network in the same manner as the messages in the subnetwork version of Figure 5.3. When they reach the dummy node "decide" at their destination, they go on to the fusion node "assemble" to wait for the other packets to arrive. Recall that a fusion node simply passes jobs without relatives, so a single packet message proceeds through to set node "ack_msg." Acknowledgements go to the sink, as before. Once all of the packets have arrived at the fusion node "assemble," the parent, representing the reassembled message, proceeds to "ack__msg."

Following is a definition of submodel "city" corresponding to Figure 5.5. It assumes that the original form of the invoking model is used, i.e., without the added node parameters used in Section 5.3. It also assumes the maximum packet size is 512 bits and that 480 of these are for data. (Thus, assuming the mean message length is 1400 bits, as before, and that 1368 of these bits are data, a message will average 2.85 packets.)

```
SUBMODEL:city
   NUMERIC PARAMETERS:city_code
   NUMERIC PARAMETERS:cw_city /*clockwise city code*/
   NUMERIC PARAMETERS:ccw_city /*counterclockwise*/
   NODE PARAMETERS:r_t
   NODE PARAMETERS:to_net_cw to_net_ccw
   NODE PARAMETERS:from_cw from_ccw
   CHAIN PARAMETERS:c
   SET NODES:msg_vals
   ASSIGNMENT LIST:jv(msg_dest)=dest_dist(city_code)   ++
                  jv(msg_leng)=msg_l_dist              ++
                  jv(msg_origin)=city_code             ++
                  jv(msg_type)=data
   SET NODES:ack_msg
   ASSIGNMENT LIST:jv(msg_dest)=jv(msg_origin)         ++
                  jv(msg_leng)=32                      ++
                  jv(msg_type)=ack
   SET NODES:dec_msg_l
   ASSIGNMENT LIST:jv(msg_leng)=jv(msg_leng)-480
   SET NODES:set_pkt_l
   ASSIGNMENT LIST:jv(msg_leng)=512
   FISSION NODES:separate
   FUSION NODES:assemble
   DUMMY NODES:decide
   CHAIN:c
      TYPE:external
      SOURCE LIST:entrance
      ARRIVAL TIMES:arrivl_tim
      /*Traffic for network: */
      :entrance->r_t->msg_vals
      :msg_vals->separate;if(jv(msg_leng)>512)
      :msg_vals->to_net_cw to_net_ccw to_net_cw to_net_ccw;  ++
       if(jv(msg_dest)=cw_city) if(jv(msg_dest)=ccw_city) .5 .5
      :separate->dec_msg_l set_pkt_l;fission
      :dec_msg_l->separate;if(jv(msg_leng)>512)
      :dec_msg_l->to_net_cw to_net_ccw to_net_cw to_net_ccw;  ++
       if(jv(msg_dest)=cw_city) if(jv(msg_dest)=ccw_city) .5 .5
      :set_pkt_l->to_net_cw to_net_ccw to_net_cw to_net_ccw;  ++
       if(jv(msg_dest)=cw_city) if(jv(msg_dest)=ccw_city) .5 .5
```

```
        /*Traffic from network: */
        :from_cw->decide to_net_cw;if(jv(msg_dest)=city_code) if(t)
        :from_ccw->decide to_net_ccw;if(jv(msg_dest)=city_code) if(t)
        :decide->sink assemble;if(jv(msg_type)=ack) if(t)
        :assemble->ack_msg
        :ack_msg->to_net_cw to_net_ccw to_net_cw to_net_ccw;  ++
         if(jv(msg_dest)=cw_city) if(jv(msg_dest)=ccw_city) .5 .5
END OF SUBMODEL CITY
```

We might get the following output from RESQ.

```
MODEL:chap5m1
RESQ2 VERSION DATE: MAY 11, 1982 - TIME: 22:04:22 DATE: 05/25/82
MEAN_LENG:1400
ARRIVL_TIM:0.20 /*used as exponential distribution with this mean*/
SAMPLING PERIOD END: RESP_TIME DEPARTURE GUIDELINE
SAMPLING PERIOD END: RESP_TIME DEPARTURE GUIDELINE
SAMPLING PERIOD END: RESP_TIME DEPARTURE GUIDELINE
NO ERRORS DETECTED DURING SIMULATION.

                SIMULATED TIME:        3050.61499
                     CPU TIME:          893.87
             NUMBER OF EVENTS:          415830
             NUMBER OF CYCLES:             257


WHAT:nd(resp_time)
INVOCATION      ELEMENT        NUMBER OF DEPARTURES
                RESP_TIME      60712
```

With the added traffic of packet control information and error correction information, we would expect the link utilizations to increase.

```
WHAT:utbo
INVOCATION      ELEMENT        UTILIZATION
                RESP_TIME      4.2024E-09(4.0927E-09,4.3120E-09) 0.0%
                NY_ATL_Q       0.58155(0.56944,0.59366) 2.4%
                ATL_DAL_Q      0.56926(0.55679,0.58173) 2.5%
                DAL_CHI_Q      0.57991(0.56802,0.59180) 2.4%
                CHI_NY_Q       0.57985(0.56772,0.59198) 2.4%
                ATL_NY_Q       0.57709(0.56568,0.58850) 2.3%
                DAL_ATL_Q      0.56969(0.55778,0.58160) 2.4%
                CHI_DAL_Q      0.58584(0.57460,0.59707) 2.2%
                NY_CHI_Q       0.58224(0.57061,0.59387) 2.3%
```

However, the mean response time decreases by roughly 70 ms.

```
WHAT:qtbo
INVOCATION      ELEMENT        MEAN QUEUEING TIME
                RESP_TIME      0.45346(0.44311,0.46381) 4.6%
```

```
                  NY_ATL_Q      0.23856(0.22194,0.25517) 13.9%
                  ATL_DAL_Q     0.22045(0.20802,0.23289) 11.3%
                  DAL_CHI_Q     0.24778(0.23274,0.26281) 12.1%
                  CHI_NY_Q      0.24809(0.22253,0.27364) 20.6%
                  ATL_NY_Q      0.22439(0.21245,0.23634) 10.6%
                  DAL_ATL_Q     0.21912(0.20795,0.23029) 10.2%
                  CHI_DAL_Q     0.23619(0.22245,0.24992) 11.6%
                  NY_CHI_Q      0.22777(0.21332,0.24222) 12.7%

WHAT:qtdbo
INVOCATION        ELEMENT       QUEUEING TIME DISTRIBUTION
                  RESP_TIME     2.00E-01:0.31649(0.31109,0.32190)  1.1%
                                4.00E-01:0.57542(0.56738,0.58346)  1.6%
                                6.00E-01:0.73524(0.72685,0.74363)  1.7%
                                8.00E-01:0.83761(0.82971,0.84551)  1.6%
                                1.00E+00:0.90099(0.89445,0.90753)  1.3%
                                1.20E+00:0.94075(0.93530,0.94621)  1.1%

WHAT:
CONTINUE RUN:no
MEAN_LENG:
```

Exercise 5.5 - Packetized Messages and Time Outs. Develop a version of the city subnetwork which incorporates packetizing of messages and time outs. The time out representation may be either the basic one of Section 5.3 or the revised one of Exercise 5.3.

5.5. ADAPTIVE ROUTING

Communication networks may be designed either with static routing, where messages from a given origin always take the same route to get to a given destination, or with dynamic routing, where different messages may be routed differently for the same (origin,destination) pair. A dynamic routing mechanism may be adaptive, trying to determine the best path given the current state of the network. The routing we have assumed so far is basically static, with the exception of the random choice of direction for messages traveling two hops. A variety of more sophisticated approaches are possible. Choice among these approaches is not clear and we will not attempt a thorough treatment of the issues here. Our focus is modeling, so we will simply illustrate how global variables might be used to maintain information for making routing decisions.

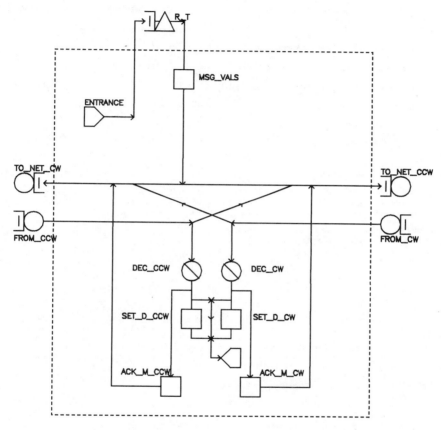

Figure 5.6 - City Submodel with Delay Statistics

The mechanism we consider is simplistic and has little effect in the small communication network we have been using as an example. The mechanism will only have an effect when a decision is needed whether a "two hop" message should be sent clockwise or counterclockwise. For two hop messages, the model records in global variables an estimate of recent delays in each direction. When a decision is needed, the direction with the lower current estimate is chosen.

Figure 5.6 illustrates a version of the city subnetwork of Figure 5.3 with the changes for this decision mechanism. The set node "msg__vals" now sets an additional job variable to the current simulated time. The dummy node "decide" has been replaced by two dummy nodes, one for each direction. Similarly, there are now two set nodes corresponding to "ack__msg." A message will go to the set node appropriate to its chosen direction to store the delay experienced getting to the destination (but not the additional delay for acknowledgement). This value is used to update the delay estimate when the acknowledgement returns to the origin. The estimate uses the exponential smoothing function $E \leftarrow .9E + .1D$, where E is the current estimate and D is the most recent delay.

We assume that the invoking model declarations now include

```
NUMERIC IDENTIFIERS:msg_dest msg_leng msg_origin msg_type msg_time
   MSG_DEST:0    /*JV(0) to be used to store destination      */
   MSG_LENG:1    /*JV(1) to be used to store length           */
   MSG_ORIGIN:2  /*JV(2) to be used to store destination      */
   MSG_TYPE:3    /*JV(3) to be used to store type, direction   */
   MSG_TIME:4    /*JV(4) to be used to store time stamp        */
NUMERIC IDENTIFIERS:ack_cw ack_ccw data
   ACK_CW:1
   ACK_CCW:2
   DATA:3
...
GLOBAL VARIABLES:clock /*simulated time special global variable*/
   CLOCK:0
MAX JV:4 /*maximum subscript*/
...
QUEUE TYPE:basic_link
   NUMERIC PARAMETERS:prop_delay
   NODE PARAMETERS:class_name
   TYPE:prty
   CLASS LIST:class_name
      SERVICE TIMES:standard(jv(msg_leng)/9600+prop_delay,0)
      PRIORITIES:max(2,jv(msg_type))
END OF QUEUE TYPE BASIC_LINK
```

Following is a RESQ definition of submodel "city."

```
SUBMODEL:city
   NUMERIC PARAMETERS:city_code
   NUMERIC PARAMETERS:cw_city /*clockwise city code*/
   NUMERIC PARAMETERS:ccw_city /*counterclockwise*/
   NODE PARAMETERS:r_t
   NODE PARAMETERS:to_net_cw to_net_ccw
```

```
NODE PARAMETERS:from_cw from_ccw
CHAIN PARAMETERS:c
GLOBAL VARIABLES:delay_cw delay_ccw temp
   DELAY_CW:.4   /*arbitrary initial estimate*/
   DELAY_CCW:.4
   TEMP:0
SET NODES:msg_vals
ASSIGNMENT LIST:jv(msg_dest)=dest_dist(city_code)   ++
               jv(msg_leng)=msg_l_dist              ++
               jv(msg_origin)=city_code             ++
               jv(msg_type)=data                    ++
               jv(msg_time)=clock
SET NODES:ack_m_cw
ASSIGNMENT LIST:temp=jv(msg_dest)                   ++
               jv(msg_dest)=jv(msg_origin)          ++
               jv(msg_origin)=temp                  ++
               jv(msg_leng)=32                      ++
               jv(msg_type)=ack_cw                  ++
               jv(msg_time)=clock-jv(msg_time)
SET NODES:ack_m_ccw
ASSIGNMENT LIST:temp=jv(msg_dest)                   ++
               jv(msg_dest)=jv(msg_origin)          ++
               jv(msg_origin)=temp                  ++
               jv(msg_leng)=32                      ++
               jv(msg_type)=ack_ccw                 ++
               jv(msg_time)=clock-jv(msg_time)
SET NODES:set_d_cw
ASSIGNMENT LIST:delay_cw=.9*delay_cw+.1*jv(msg_time)
SET NODES:set_d_ccw
ASSIGNMENT LIST:delay_ccw=.9*delay_ccw+.1*jv(msg_time)
DUMMY NODES:dec_cw dec_ccw
CHAIN:c
   TYPE:external
   SOURCE LIST:entrance
   ARRIVAL TIMES:arrivl_tim
   /*Traffic for network: */
   :entrance->r_t->msg_vals
   :msg_vals->to_net_cw to_net_ccw to_net_cw to_net_ccw;   ++
    if(jv(msg_dest)=cw_city) if(jv(msg_dest)=ccw_city)     ++
    if(delay_cw<delay_ccw)    if(t)
   /*Traffic from network: */
   :from_cw->dec_cw to_net_cw;if(jv(msg_dest)=city_code) if(t)
   :from_ccw->dec_ccw to_net_ccw;if(jv(msg_dest)=city_code) if(t)
   :dec_cw->ack_m_cw;if(jv(msg_type)=data)
   :dec_cw->sink;if(abs(jv(msg_dest)-jv(msg_origin))=1)
   :dec_cw->set_d_cw set_d_ccw;if(jv(msg_type)=ack_cw) if(t)
   :ack_m_cw->to_net_cw to_net_ccw to_net_cw to_net_ccw;   ++
    if(jv(msg_dest)=cw_city) if(jv(msg_dest)=ccw_city) .5 .5
   :dec_ccw->ack_m_ccw;if(jv(msg_type)=data)
   :dec_ccw->sink;if(abs(jv(msg_dest)-jv(msg_origin))=1)
   :dec_ccw->set_d_cw set_d_ccw;if(jv(msg_type)=ack_cw) if(t)
   :set_d_cw set_d_ccw->sink
   :ack_m_ccw->to_net_cw to_net_ccw to_net_cw to_net_ccw; ++
```

```
        if(jv(msg_dest)=cw_city) if(jv(msg_dest)=ccw_city) .5 .5
END OF SUBMODEL CITY
```

Unlike previous versions, this submodel sets the origin of an acknowledgement properly, so that it may be determined whether or not the message is a two hop message.

We might get the following results from RESQ.

```
MODEL:chap5m3
RESQ2 VERSION DATE: MAY 27, 1982 - TIME: 23:39:12 DATE: 05/30/82
MEAN_LENG:1400
ARRIVL_TIM:0.20 /*used as exponential distribution with this mean*/
WARNING -- MODEL MAY NOT BE TRULY REGENERATIVE
               BECAUSE OF USE OF GLOBAL VARIABLES
SAMPLING PERIOD END: RESP_TIME DEPARTURE GUIDELINE
SAMPLING PERIOD END: RESP_TIME DEPARTURE GUIDELINE
NO ERRORS DETECTED DURING SIMULATION.

                    SIMULATED TIME:      2042.38135
                         CPU TIME:         333.53
                 NUMBER OF EVENTS:         149375
                 NUMBER OF CYCLES:            126

WHAT:nd(resp_time)
INVOCATION        ELEMENT        NUMBER OF DEPARTURES
                  RESP_TIME      40689

WHAT:utbo
INVOCATION        ELEMENT        UTILIZATION
                  RESP_TIME      4.9662E-09(4.8230E-09,5.1093E-09) 0.0%
                  NY_ATL_Q       0.52618(0.51044,0.54192) 3.1%
                  ATL_DAL_Q      0.51254(0.49596,0.52912) 3.3%
                  DAL_CHI_Q      0.52512(0.50674,0.54350) 3.7%
                  CHI_NY_Q       0.52963(0.51104,0.54822) 3.7%
                  ATL_NY_Q       0.52298(0.50184,0.54411) 4.2%
                  DAL_ATL_Q      0.51182(0.49116,0.53248) 4.1%
                  CHI_DAL_Q      0.52263(0.50661,0.53864) 3.2%
                  NY_CHI_Q       0.53618(0.52191,0.55045) 2.9%

WHAT:qtbo
INVOCATION        ELEMENT        MEAN QUEUEING TIME
                  RESP_TIME      0.53531(0.52243,0.54820) 4.8%
                  NY_ATL_Q       0.20246(0.19197,0.21295) 10.4%
                  ATL_DAL_Q      0.19758(0.18617,0.20899) 11.5%
                  DAL_CHI_Q      0.21389(0.20012,0.22765) 12.9%
                  CHI_NY_Q       0.20141(0.18707,0.21575) 14.2%
                  ATL_NY_Q       0.19740(0.18635,0.20846) 11.2%
                  DAL_ATL_Q      0.18621(0.17505,0.19738) 12.0%
                  CHI_DAL_Q      0.20227(0.19032,0.21422) 11.8%
```

```
                    NY_CHI_Q          0.20208(0.19148,0.21268) 10.5%

WHAT:qtdbo
INVOCATION          ELEMENT           QUEUEING TIME DISTRIBUTION
                    RESP_TIME         2.00E-01:0.25398(0.24765,0.26030)  1.3%
                                      4.00E-01:0.49633(0.48775,0.50490)  1.7%
                                      6.00E-01:0.66853(0.65854,0.67853)  2.0%
                                      8.00E-01:0.78247(0.77340,0.79154)  1.8%
                                      1.00E+00:0.85795(0.84992,0.86598)  1.6%
                                      1.20E+00:0.90801(0.90088,0.91513)  1.4%


WHAT:gv
INVOCATION          ELEMENT           FINAL VALUES OF GLOBAL VARIABLES
                    CLOCK             2042.38135
NEW_YORK            DELAY_CW          1.72158
NEW_YORK            DELAY_CCW         0.21239
NEW_YORK            TEMP              1.00000
ATLANTA             DELAY_CW          0.62367
ATLANTA             DELAY_CCW         2.02729
ATLANTA             TEMP              2.00000
DALLAS              DELAY_CW          1.15409
DALLAS              DELAY_CCW         1.94663
DALLAS              TEMP              3.00000
CHICAGO             DELAY_CW          0.73166
CHICAGO             DELAY_CCW         1.35357
CHICAGO             TEMP              4.00000

WHAT:
CONTINUE RUN:no
MEAN_LENG:
```

As we would expect, the results are essentially the same as before.

Exercise 5.6 - Quadratic Adaptive Routing. Agnew [1] has suggested that adaptive routing decisions be based on a function of the form $(1+L)(1+L/2)$, where L is the current estimate of the total queue length along a path being considered. Develop a version of the city subnetwork using such a routing mechanism. Normally estimates used in adaptive routing decisions, e.g., the queue lengths required here, will be based on periodic updates furnished by adjacent nodes. You may need not represent these updates.

Exercise 5.7 - Routing Estimate Updating. In Exercise 5.6 add the updating messages required for the queue length estimates.

5.6. FLOW CONTROL

Often it is important to limit the number of messages in transit between a sender and a recipient. The sender may be able to generate messages much more rapidly than the recipient can handle them. If the sequence of messages is important, as it usually is, having many messages in transit runs a risk of intermediate messages in the sequence being lost, causing either excess retransmission or excess buffering. The limits may be imposed between neighboring nodes in the communication network, or between ends of a virtual circuit, or both.

A common limiting mechanism is "window" flow control. A sender has a window, i.e., a limit, to the number of messages which may be sent before the recipient explicity requests that more messages be sent. Two basic varieties are fixed window and variable window protocols. In a fixed window protocol the recipient waits until the entire window has been received before requesting a new window. The simplest fixed window protocol would be to have a window size of one and require that the sender wait for an acknowledgement before sending the next message. In a variable window protocol, the recipient requests additional messages before receiving all of the messages of the last window, e.g., after receiving the first message of the last window. This allows time for the request to get back to the sender, allowing a more continuous flow.

Figure 5.7 suggests the additions to the subnetwork of Figure 5.3 to represent variable window flow control from the represented city to each of the possible destinations. A global variable ("count__cw," "count__ccw" or "count__two") is used to count the generated messages, modulo the window size. When the count is zero, the generated message is considered the first message of a new window and a job variable ("rep__bit") is set to indicate that this message should eventually generate a reply asking for a new window. (The acknowledgement will function as this reply when the bit is set.) All generated messages wait for a token of the appropriate

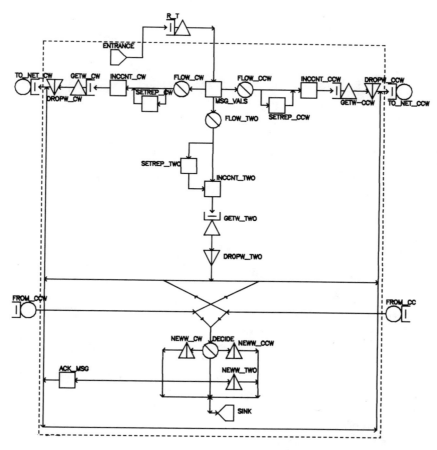

Figure 5.7 - City Submodel with Flow Control

passive queue (depending on destination) before proceeding. Once a message gets a window token, it destroys it and proceeds as before. An acknowledgement with the reply bit set will generate a new window of tokens.

Following is the revised definition of submodel "city" with the additions for window flow control.

```
SUBMODEL:city
   NUMERIC PARAMETERS:city_code
   NUMERIC PARAMETERS:cw_city /*clockwise city code*/
   NUMERIC PARAMETERS:ccw_city /*counterclockwise*/
   NODE PARAMETERS:r_t
   NODE PARAMETERS:to_net_cw to_net_ccw
   NODE PARAMETERS:from_cw from_ccw
   CHAIN PARAMETERS:c
   NUMERIC IDENTIFIERS:windowsize
      WINDOWSIZE:2
   GLOBAL VARIABLES:count_cw count_ccw count_two/*hops*/
      COUNT_CW:0
      COUNT_CCW:0
      COUNT_TWO:0
   QUEUE:wind_cwq
      TYPE:passive
      TOKENS:windowsize
      DSPL:fcfs
      ALLOCATE NODE LIST:getw_cw
         NUMBERS OF TOKENS TO ALLOCATE:1
      DESTROY NODE LIST:dropw_cw
      CREATE NODE LIST:neww_cw
         NUMBERS OF TOKENS TO CREATE:windowsize
   QUEUE:wind_ccwq
      TYPE:passive
      TOKENS:windowsize
      DSPL:fcfs
      ALLOCATE NODE LIST:getw_ccw
         NUMBERS OF TOKENS TO ALLOCATE:1
      DESTROY NODE LIST:dropw_ccw
      CREATE NODE LIST:neww_ccw
         NUMBERS OF TOKENS TO CREATE:windowsize
   QUEUE:wind_twoq
      TYPE:passive
      TOKENS:windowsize
      DSPL:fcfs
      ALLOCATE NODE LIST:getw_two
         NUMBERS OF TOKENS TO ALLOCATE:1
      DESTROY NODE LIST:dropw_two
      CREATE NODE LIST:neww_two
         NUMBERS OF TOKENS TO CREATE:windowsize
   SET NODES:msg_vals
   ASSIGNMENT LIST:jv(msg_dest)=dest_dist(city_code)   ++
                   jv(msg_leng)=msg_l_dist             ++
                   jv(msg_origin)=city_code            ++
                   jv(msg_type)=data
   SET NODES:ack_msg
   ASSIGNMENT LIST:temp=jv(msg_dest)                   ++
                   jv(msg_dest)=jv(msg_origin)         ++
                   jv(msg_origin)=temp                 ++
                   jv(msg_leng)=32                     ++
                   jv(msg_type)=ack
   SET NODES:inccnt_cw
```

```
     ASSIGNMENT LIST:count_cw=(count_cw+1) mod windowsize
     SET NODES:inccnt_ccw
     ASSIGNMENT LIST:count_ccw=(count_ccw+1) mod windowsize
     SET NODES:inccnt_two
     ASSIGNMENT LIST:count_two=(count_two+1) mod windowsize
     SET NODES:setrep_cw setrep_ccw setrep_two
     ASSIGNMENT LIST:jv(rep_bit)=1 jv(rep_bit)=1 jv(rep_bit)=1
     DUMMY NODES:decide flow_cw flow_ccw flow_two
     CHAIN:c
        TYPE:external
        SOURCE LIST:entrance
        ARRIVAL TIMES:arrivl_tim
        /*Traffic for network: */
        :entrance->r_t->msg_vals
        :msg_vals->flow_cw flow_ccw flow_two; ++
         if(jv(msg_dest)=cw_city) if(jv(msg_dest)=ccw_city) if(t)
        :flow_cw->setrep_cw inccnt_cw;if(count_cw=0) if(t)
        :setrep_cw->inccnt_cw->getw_cw->dropw_cw->to_net_cw
        :flow_ccw->setrep_ccw inccnt_ccw;if(count_ccw=0) if(t)
        :setrep_ccw->inccnt_ccw->getw_ccw->dropw_ccw->to_net_ccw
        :flow_two->setrep_two inccnt_two;if(count_two=0) if(t)
        :setrep_two->inccnt_two->getw_two->dropw_two
        :dropw_two->to_net_cw to_net_ccw;.5 .5
        /*Traffic from network: */
        :from_cw->decide to_net_cw;if(jv(msg_dest)=city_code) if(t)
        :from_ccw->decide to_net_ccw;if(jv(msg_dest)=city_code) if(t)
        :decide->ack_msg;if(jv(msg_type)=data)
        :ack_msg->to_net_cw to_net_ccw to_net_cw to_net_ccw; ++
         if(jv(msg_dest)=cw_city) if(jv(msg_dest)=ccw_city) .5 .5
        :decide->sink;if(jv(rep_bit)=0)
        :decide->neww_cw;if(jv(msg_origin)=cw_city)
        :decide->neww_ccw;if(jv(msg_origin)=ccw_city)
        :decide->neww_two;if(t)
        :neww_cw neww_ccw neww_two->sink
END OF SUBMODEL CITY
```

With a window size of two, there can be at most three messages outstanding between a given sender and recipient, the last message of the last window and the two messages of the current window. The definition of the invoking model is the same as we gave in Section 5.1 except for the additional identifier declaration ("rep__bit") and the increase of "MAX JV". We get the following results from running the simulation:

```
RESQ2 VERSION DATE: JUNE 11, 1982 -  TIME: 17:39:36  DATE: 06/16/82
MODEL:CHAP5M4
MEAN_LENG:1400
ARRIVL_TIM:0.20 /*used as exponential distribution with this mean*/
WARNING -- MODEL MAY NOT BE TRULY REGENERATIVE
             BECAUSE OF USE OF GLOBAL VARIABLES
```

The above warning is given because RESQ does not attempt to verify that global variables have the same values at each occurrence of what appears to be the regeneration state. In this model the global variables will always be zero in the empty system state, so the model is truly regenerative.

```
SAMPLING PERIOD END: RESP_TIME DEPARTURE GUIDELINE
SAMPLING PERIOD END: RESP_TIME DEPARTURE GUIDELINE
SAMPLING PERIOD END: RESP_TIME DEPARTURE GUIDELINE
SAMPLING PERIOD END: RESP_TIME DEPARTURE GUIDELINE
SAMPLING PERIOD END: RESP_TIME DEPARTURE GUIDELINE
NO ERRORS DETECTED DURING SIMULATION.
```

SIMULATED TIME:	5085.95703
CPU TIME:	944.37
NUMBER OF EVENTS:	373063
NUMBER OF CYCLES:	195

```
WHAT:nd
INVOCATION        ELEMENT        NUMBER OF DEPARTURES
                  RESP_TIME      101613
                  NY_ATL_Q       33831
                  ATL_DAL_Q      33798
                  DAL_CHI_Q      33866
                  CHI_NY_Q       34004
                  ATL_NY_Q       33944
                  DAL_ATL_Q      33911
                  CHI_DAL_Q      33979
                  NY_CHI_Q       34117
NEW_YORK          WIND_CWQ       8395
NEW_YORK          WIND_CCWQ      8378
NEW_YORK          WIND_TWOQ      8564
ATLANTA           WIND_CWQ       8421
ATLANTA           WIND_CCWQ      8475
ATLANTA           WIND_TWOQ      8438
DALLAS            WIND_CWQ       8528
DALLAS            WIND_CCWQ      8433
DALLAS            WIND_TWOQ      8597
CHICAGO           WIND_CWQ       8571
CHICAGO           WIND_CCWQ      8300
CHICAGO           WIND_TWOQ      8513
NEW_YORK          DROPW_CW       8395


...


                  SINK           101613


WHAT:utbo
INVOCATION        ELEMENT        UTILIZATION
                  RESP_TIME      5.8983E-09(5.7389E-09,6.0577E-09) 0.0%
```

```
                    NY_ATL_Q       0.52487(0.51579,0.53394) 1.8%
                    ATL_DAL_Q      0.51688(0.50799,0.52576) 1.8%
                    DAL_CHI_Q      0.52163(0.51251,0.53076) 1.8%
                    CHI_NY_Q       0.52163(0.51180,0.53147) 2.0%
                    ATL_NY_Q       0.52367(0.51422,0.53312) 1.9%
                    DAL_ATL_Q      0.52452(0.51493,0.53411) 1.9%
                    CHI_DAL_Q      0.52510(0.51521,0.53499) 2.0%
                    NY_CHI_Q       0.52878(0.51940,0.53817) 1.9%


...


WHAT:qtbo(*)
INVOCATION          ELEMENT        MEAN QUEUEING TIME
                    RESP_TIME      0.63398(0.61814,0.64982) 5.0%
                     NY_R_T         0.64396(0.61909,0.66883) 7.7%
                     ATL_R_T        0.62706(0.60562,0.64850) 6.8%
                     DAL_R_T        0.63684(0.60256,0.67112) 10.8%
                     CHI_R_T        0.62806(0.60843,0.64769) 6.3%
                    NY_ATL_Q       0.18235(0.17792,0.18678) 4.9%
                    ATL_DAL_Q      0.17970(0.17511,0.18430) 5.1%
                    DAL_CHI_Q      0.18239(0.17769,0.18709) 5.2%
                    CHI_NY_Q       0.18134(0.17576,0.18692) 6.2%
                    ATL_NY_Q       0.18063(0.17541,0.18585) 5.8%
                    DAL_ATL_Q      0.18392(0.17897,0.18886) 5.4%
                    CHI_DAL_Q      0.18263(0.17717,0.18810) 6.0%
                    NY_CHI_Q       0.18515(0.18083,0.18947) 4.7%
NEW_YORK            WIND_CWQ       0.03528(0.02909,0.04146) 35.1%
NEW_YORK            WIND_CCWQ      0.03307(0.02765,0.03848) 32.8%
NEW_YORK            WIND_TWOQ      0.39271(0.33482,0.45060) 29.5%
ATLANTA             WIND_CWQ       0.03474(0.02883,0.04066) 34.0%
ATLANTA             WIND_CCWQ      0.03857(0.03041,0.04672) 42.3%
ATLANTA             WIND_TWOQ      0.35275(0.30643,0.39908) 26.3%
DALLAS              WIND_CWQ       0.03352(0.02883,0.03822) 28.0%
DALLAS              WIND_CCWQ      0.03700(0.03149,0.04251) 29.8%
DALLAS              WIND_TWOQ      0.37693(0.29218,0.46169) 45.0%
CHICAGO             WIND_CWQ       0.04030(0.02863,0.05197) 57.9%
CHICAGO             WIND_CCWQ      0.03495(0.02978,0.04012) 29.6%
CHICAGO             WIND_TWOQ      0.34516(0.30665,0.38367) 22.3%

WHAT:qtdbo
INVOCATION          ELEMENT        QUEUEING TIME DISTRIBUTION
                    RESP_TIME      2.00E-01:0.24422(0.24065,0.24779) 0.7%
                                   4.00E-01:0.47451(0.46899,0.48003) 1.1%
                                   6.00E-01:0.63528(0.62916,0.64141) 1.2%
                                   8.00E-01:0.74401(0.73796,0.75005) 1.2%
                                   1.00E+00:0.81620(0.81040,0.82201) 1.2%
                                   1.20E+00:0.86623(0.86071,0.87175) 1.1%

WHAT:
CONTINUE RUN:no
MEAN_LENG:
```

CHAPTER 6

LOCAL AREA NETWORKS

So far our models have presumably dealt with at least moderate sized computers and have left unresolved issues with regard to how terminals and other workstations fit into the picture. In this chapter we consider local networks explicitly. The discussion applies both to local networks independent of long haul networks and to local networks as sources of traffic carried by long haul networks. We consider representation of the traditional approach of polled multidrop lines and of two more recent approaches, CSMA/CD (carrier sense multiple access with collision detection) networks and token rings.

6.1. POLLING PROTOCOLS

Until recently, polling has been the dominant protocol for connection of several stations on a single communication line. One station, i.e., a line controller, regulates the use of the line by other stations, e.g., terminals. The controlling station asks each other station, in turn, whether it has any traffic. This is done by sending a polling message to that station. The station either proceeds to send messages it has been holding or replies that it has no traffic. The polling normally is sequential among the stations, but other orders are used in some systems to favor some stations over others.

We will consider a system of ten terminals on a full duplex 2400 baud line. With probability 0.5 a terminal generated message will be destined for a station across a long haul network, e.g., a network of the sort we have considered in previous chapters. Our model does not represent the long haul network, but simply assumes that the time for a message to get across the long haul network and produce a reply has an exponential distribution with mean 1.5 seconds. With probability 0.5 a terminal generated message will be destined for another of the terminals on the same line, each of the other terminals being equally likely. In this case, the receiving terminal will

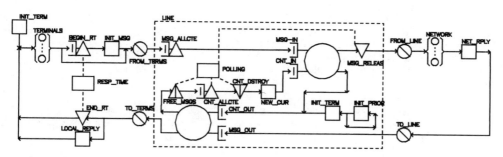

Figure 6.1 - Polling of Terminals

generate a reply to be sent back to the terminal generating the original message. Figure 6.1 depicts this model.

Following is a submodel definition for the submodel representing the controller. (Some of the identifiers are declared in the invoking model.)

```
SUBMODEL:poll_line
   NUMERIC PARAMETERS:no_terms
   NODE PARAMETERS:from_terms from_line to_line to_terms
   CHAIN PARAMETERS:c
   GLOBAL VARIABLES:cur_term cur_prior(no_terms)
      CUR_TERM:1
```

```
        CUR_PRIOR:0
     QUEUE:polling
        TYPE:passive
        TOKENS:0
        DSPL:prty
        ALLOCATE NODE LIST:msg_allcte
           NUMBERS OF TOKENS TO ALLOCATE:1
           PRIORITIES:cur_prior(jv(msg_origin))
        ALLOCATE NODE LIST:cnt_allcte
           NUMBERS OF TOKENS TO ALLOCATE:1
           PRIORITIES:cur_prior(cur_term)+1
        RELEASE NODE LIST:msg_releas
        DESTROY NODE LIST:cnt_dstroy
        CREATE NODE LIST:free_msgs
           NUMBERS OF TOKENS TO CREATE:1
     QUEUE:to_net
        TYPE:fcfs
        CLASS LIST:msg_in
           SERVICE TIMES:standard(jv(msg_leng)/2400,0)
        CLASS LIST:cnt_in
           SERVICE TIMES:standard(16/2400,0)
     QUEUE:from_net
        TYPE:prty
        CLASS LIST:msg_out
           SERVICE TIMES:standard(jv(msg_leng)/2400,0)
           PRIORITIES:2
        CLASS LIST:cnt_out
           SERVICE TIMES:standard(16/2400,0)
           PRIORITIES:1
     SET NODES:new_cur
     ASSIGNMENT LIST:cur_prior(cur_term)=                    ++
                         cur_prior(cur_term)+2*no_terms   ++
                 cur_term=(cur_term mod no_terms)+1
     SET NODES:init_prior
     ASSIGNMENT LIST:cur_prior(cur_term)=cur_term*2-1         ++
                 cur_term=cur_term+1
     SET NODES:init_term
     ASSIGNMENT LIST:cur_term=1
     CHAIN:c
        TYPE:external
        :from_terms->msg_allcte->msg_in->msg_releas->from_line
        :to_line->msg_out->to_terms
     CHAIN:pollingjob
        TYPE:closed
        POPULATION:1
        :init_prior->init_prior;if(cur_term<=no_terms)
        :init_prior->init_term;if(t)
        :init_term->cnt_out->free_msgs->cnt_allcte->cnt_dstroy
        :cnt_dstroy->new_cur->cnt_in->cnt_out
END OF SUBMODEL POLL_LINE
```

The polling is represented by the priority scheduling of the passive queue "polling." A job representing the polling message changes the priorities of the terminals in order. The routing chain for the polling job is contained entirely within the submodel, unlike chains in other submodels we have used. The polling message is assumed to be 16 bits long, and propagation delays are assumed insignificant because of relatively short distances.

When a terminal is being polled, it will have highest priority. The polling message will have priority one lower than the data messages for the polled terminal. The polling job creates a token and then waits to get the token. Messages from the polled terminal get the token, experience a transmission delay and return the token. When the polled terminal has no messages, the polling job gets the token, destroys it, resets the priorities, experiences transmission delays and then creates another token. The model does not recycle priority values, since the possible values will not be exhausted in any feasible run length. However, it would be possible to reset the values if that were necessary.

Following is a definition of the model invoking this polling representation.

```
MODEL:chap6m1
   METHOD:simulation
   NUMERIC IDENTIFIERS:no_terms thinktime
      NO_TERMS:10
      THINKTIME:10
   NUMERIC IDENTIFIERS:msg_dest msg_leng msg_origin terminal
      MSG_DEST:0     /*JV to be used to indicate destination*/
      MSG_LENG:1     /*JV to be used to indicate length     */
      MSG_ORIGIN:2   /*JV to be used to indicate origin     */
      TERMINAL:3     /*JV to be used to indicate terminal   */
   GLOBAL VARIABLES:temp
      TEMP:0
   MAX JV:3
   QUEUE:terminalsq
      TYPE:is
      CLASS LIST:terminals
         SERVICE TIMES:thinktime
   QUEUE:resp_time /*response time*/
      TYPE:passive
      TOKENS:2147483647 /*"infinity"*/
      DSPL:fcfs
      ALLOCATE NODE LIST:begin_rt
         NUMBERS OF TOKENS TO ALLOCATE:1
      RELEASE NODE LIST: end_rt
```

```
QUEUE:networkq
   TYPE:is
   CLASS LIST:network
      SERVICE TIMES:1.5
SET NODES:init_term
   ASSIGNMENT LIST:temp=temp+1 jv(terminal)=temp
SET NODES:init_msg
   ASSIGNMENT LIST:                                              ++
   jv(msg_leng)=standard(800,1)                                  ++
   jv(msg_origin)=jv(terminal)                                   ++
   jv(msg_dest)=ceil(uniform(0,0,0.5;                            ++
    0,jv(terminal)-1,(jv(terminal)-1)/2*(no_terms-1);            ++
      jv(terminal),no_terms,(no_terms-jv(terminal))/2*(no_terms-1)))
SET NODES:net_reply
   ASSIGNMENT LIST:                                              ++
   jv(msg_leng)=standard(800,1)                                  ++
   jv(msg_origin)=jv(terminal)                                   ++
   jv(msg_dest)=jv(terminal)
SET NODES:local_rply
   ASSIGNMENT LIST:                                              ++
   jv(msg_leng)=standard(800,1)                                  ++
   jv(msg_origin)=jv(msg_dest)                                   ++
   jv(msg_dest)=jv(terminal)
DUMMY NODES:from_terms from_line to_line to_terms
INCLUDE:poll
INVOCATION:line
   TYPE:poll_line
   NO_TERMS:no_terms
   FROM_TERMS:from_terms
   FROM_LINE:from_line
   TO_LINE:to_line
   TO_TERMS:to_terms
   C:c
CHAIN:c
   TYPE:closed
   POPULATION:no_terms
   :terminals->begin_rt from_terms;                             ++
            if(th(resp_time)=0) if(t)
   :begin_rt->init_msg->from_terms
   :from_line->to_line network;if(jv(msg_dest)>0) if(t)
   :network->net_reply->to_line
   :to_terms->end_rt local_rply;                                ++
            if(jv(msg_dest)=jv(terminal)) if(t)
   :end_rt local_rply->terminals
  /*initialization of terminals*/
   :init_term->terminals
QUEUES FOR QUEUEING TIME DIST:resp_time
   VALUES:.5 1 2 4 8
CONFIDENCE INTERVAL METHOD:spectral
INITIAL STATE DEFINITION-
CHAIN:line.pollingjob
   NODE LIST:line.init_prior
   INIT POP:1
```

```
CHAIN:c
   NODE LIST:init_term
   INIT POP: no_terms
CONFIDENCE LEVEL:90
SEQUENTIAL STOPPING RULE:yes
   CONFIDENCE INTERVAL QUEUES:resp_time resp_time
      MEASURES:                  qt        qtd
      ALLOWED WIDTHS:            10        10
INITIAL PORTION DISCARDED:10
INITIAL PERIOD LIMITS-
   QUEUES FOR DEPARTURE COUNTS:resp_time
      DEPARTURES:1000
LIMIT - CP SECONDS:1000
TRACE:no
END
```

The "terminal" job variable always indicates the "home" of the message, i.e., a job which represents a reply will have its "msg_origin" job variable indicating the identity of the replying terminal, but the "terminal" job variable will still be the identity of the message originator. Destination zero is used to indicate traffic for a station across the long haul network. The RESQ "uniform" distribution is an extension of the classical uniform distribution to allow several disjoint intervals. Each interval is specified by a triple giving the lower bound, the upper bound and the probability of that interval.

Following are results from running this model:

```
RESQ2 VERSION DATE: JUNE 11, 1982 -  TIME: 17:14:04  DATE: 06/16/82
MODEL:CHAP6M1
ERROR: WARNING - NODE NOT BRANCHED TO: INIT_TERM
SAMPLING PERIOD END: RESP_TIME DEPARTURE LIMIT
SAMPLING PERIOD END: RESP_TIME DEPARTURE LIMIT
SAMPLING PERIOD END: RESP_TIME DEPARTURE LIMIT
NO ERRORS DETECTED DURING SIMULATION.  12578 DISCARDED EVENTS

                SIMULATED TIME:      3558.08154
                     CPU TIME:          417.37
              NUMBER OF EVENTS:         257844

WHAT:nd(resp_time,line.polling)
INVOCATION      ELEMENT          NUMBER OF DEPARTURES
                RESP_TIME        2025
LINE            POLLING          126900
LINE            RELEASE          3015
LINE            DESTROY          123885
```

```
WHAT:ut(line.msg_in,line.cnt_in,line.msg_out,line.cnt_out)
INVOCATION      ELEMENT      UTILIZATION
LINE            MSG_IN         0.28164
LINE            CNT_IN         0.23212
LINE            MSG_OUT        0.28115
LINE            CNT_OUT        0.23212


WHAT:qt(*)
INVOCATION      ELEMENT      MEAN QUEUEING TIME
                RESP_TIME    7.70193(7.40312,8.00074)  7.8%
                TERMINALSQ   10.01314
                NETWORKQ     1.48203
LINE            POLLING      0.02907
LINE            MSG_ALLCTE     0.89098
LINE            CNT_ALLCTE     8.0890E-03
LINE              RELEASE    0.89189
LINE              DESTROY    8.0890E-03
LINE            TO_NET       0.01441
LINE            MSG_IN         0.33237
LINE            CNT_IN         6.6667E-03
LINE            FROM_NET     0.02266
LINE            MSG_OUT        0.38003
LINE            CNT_OUT        0.01397


WHAT:qtdbo
INVOCATION      ELEMENT      QUEUEING TIME DISTRIBUTION
                RESP_TIME    5.00E-01:0.01136(0.00750,0.01521)  0.8%
                             1.00E+00:0.06074(0.05037,0.07111)  2.1%
                             2.00E+00:0.22765(0.21534,0.23997)  2.5%
                             4.00E+00:0.48296(0.46058,0.50535)  4.5%
                             8.00E+00:0.70272(0.69002,0.71541)  2.5%


WHAT:
CONTINUE RUN:no
```

Exercise 6.1 - Polling representation. The representation
of polling used in this model is expensive in terms of
simulated events, because of the polling that occurs when
there are no waiting messages. (In the simulation above,
there were only 3015 data messages transmitted from the
terminals, but there were 123885 polling messages transmitted from the terminals.) How would you refine this
model to reduce this expense?

6.2. CSMA/CD PROTOCOLS

In recent years, much attention has been paid to local area networks using CSMA/CD (carrier sense multiple access with collision detection) protocols, such as the one used in the Xerox Ethernet[TM]. Such networks typically use a coaxial cable connecting the stations on the network. The cable is strung from station to station with a total length on the order of one kilometer. The data rate is usually in the range of 1-10 megabits per second. Each station monitors the cable to see if there is traffic (a carrier) on the cable. When a station wishes to transmit, it waits until the cable is idle and then initiates transmission. However, because of propagation delays, two or more stations may still try to use the cable at the same time. The interference between the attempted simultaneous transmissions (a destructive collision) is detected by each station because the station is monitoring the cable to verify that what it "hears" is what it is transmitting. When a station recognizes a collision, it stops its transmission and waits a random time interval before trying again. (Other mechanisms besides a random wait are also used in some protocols.)

Figure 6.2 depicts an extended queueing network representation of a CSMA/CD local area network. The stations representing both the terminals and the connection to the long haul network in this example have the same characteristics as in the polling example of the last section. A binary valued global variable "collision" is used to indicate whether a collision is currently occurring or not. Passive queue "cable" represents contention for the cable. Active queue "timing" has two classes, one for the propagation delay and the other for the delay due to data rate. When the cable is idle an arriving job gets the cable token and experiences a propagation delay. If another job arrives during the propagation delay, it sets the collision variable to indicate a collision has occurred. If another job arrives while the cable is in use but after the propagation delay, it simply waits for the cable to be free. After a job finishes its propagation delay, if it determines that no collision occurs, then it proceeds to the class representing the remainder of its transmission time. If there was a collision, then it releases the cable and goes to a class representing the delay before retry. The other jobs waiting for the cable token (which actually were involved in the collision) release the cable token immediately and go to the retry class. The very last of these also clears the collision variable.

Following is a RESQ definition of the submodel representing the CSMA/CD protocol:

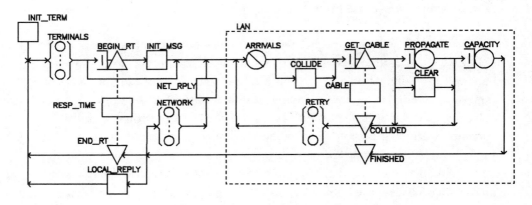

Figure 6.2 - CSMA/CD Representation

```
SUBMODEL:csma_cd
   CHAIN PARAMETERS:c
   GLOBAL VARIABLES:collision
      COLLISION:0
   QUEUE:cable
      TYPE:passive
      TOKENS:1
      DSPL:fcfs
      ALLOCATE NODE LIST:get_cable
         NUMBERS OF TOKENS TO ALLOCATE:1
      RELEASE NODE LIST:collided finished
   QUEUE:timing
      TYPE:fcfs
      CLASS LIST:propagate
         SERVICE TIMES:standard(1/3.0E+05,0)
```

```
        CLASS LIST:capacity
           SERVICE TIMES:standard(jv(msg_leng)/1.0E+06,0)
     QUEUE:retryq
        TYPE:is
        CLASS LIST:retry
           SERVICE TIMES:2000/1.0E+06
     SET NODES:collide clear
        ASSIGNMENT LIST:collision=1 collision=0
     DUMMY NODES:arrivals
     CHAIN:c
        TYPE:external
        INPUT:arrivals
        OUTPUT:finished
        :arrivals->get_cable collide;if(ql(propagate)=0) if(t)
        :collide->get_cable
        :get_cable->propagate clear collided; ++
                 if(collision=0) if(ql(get_cable)=1) if(t)
        :propagate->capacity collided; ++
                 if(collision=0) if(t)
        :capacity->finished
        :clear->collided
        :collided->retry->arrivals
END OF SUBMODEL CSMA_CD
```

This definition assumes the cable length is exactly one kilometer and that the data rate is one megabit per second. The retry delay is exponential with mean equal to the transmission delay for two and a half messages.

Following is the model invoking the CSMA/CD submodel. Up until the submodel inclusion it is the same as the model used for the polling example.

```
MODEL:chap6m2
   METHOD:simulation
   NUMERIC IDENTIFIERS:no_terms thinktime
      NO_TERMS:10
      THINKTIME:10
   NUMERIC IDENTIFIERS:msg_dest msg_leng msg_origin terminal
      MSG_DEST:0    /*JV to be used to indicate destination*/
      MSG_LENG:1    /*JV to be used to indicate length     */
      MSG_ORIGIN:2  /*JV to be used to indicate origin     */
      TERMINAL:3    /*JV to be used to indicate terminal   */
   GLOBAL VARIABLES:temp
      TEMP:0
   MAX JV:3
   QUEUE:terminalsq
      TYPE:is
      CLASS LIST:terminals
         SERVICE TIMES:thinktime
   QUEUE:resp_time /*response time*/
```

```
      TYPE:passive
      TOKENS:2147483647 /*"infinity"*/
      DSPL:fcfs
      ALLOCATE NODE LIST:begin_rt
          NUMBERS OF TOKENS TO ALLOCATE:1
      RELEASE NODE LIST: end_rt
   QUEUE:networkq
      TYPE:is
      CLASS LIST:network
          SERVICE TIMES:1.5
   SET NODES:init_term
      ASSIGNMENT LIST:temp=temp+1 jv(terminal)=temp
   SET NODES:init_msg
      ASSIGNMENT LIST:                                              ++
      jv(msg_leng)=standard(800,1)                                  ++
      jv(msg_origin)=jv(terminal)                                   ++
      jv(msg_dest)=ceil(uniform(0,0,0.5;                            ++
       0,jv(terminal)-1,(jv(terminal)-1)/2*(no_terms-1);           ++
       jv(terminal),no_terms,(no_terms-jv(terminal))/2*(no_terms-1)))
   SET NODES:net_reply
      ASSIGNMENT LIST:                                              ++
      jv(msg_leng)=standard(800,1)                                  ++
      jv(msg_origin)=jv(terminal)                                   ++
      jv(msg_dest)=jv(terminal)
   SET NODES:local_rply
      ASSIGNMENT LIST:                                              ++
      jv(msg_leng)=standard(800,1)                                  ++
      jv(msg_origin)=jv(msg_dest)                                   ++
      jv(msg_dest)=jv(terminal)
```

Because the submodel itself is simpler than the polling submodel, the invocation and connections are also simpler.

```
   INCLUDE:csma_cd
   INVOCATION:lan
      TYPE:csma_cd
      C:c
   CHAIN:c
      TYPE:closed
      POPULATION:no_terms
      :terminals->begin_rt lan.input;                              ++
               if(th(resp_time)=0) if(t)
      :begin_rt->init_msg->lan.input
      :lan.output->network;if(jv(msg_dest)=0)
      :lan.output->network end_rt local_rply;                      ++
       if(jv(msg_dest)=0) if(jv(msg_dest)=jv(terminal)) if(t)
      :network->net_reply->lan.input
      :end_rt local_rply >terminals
    /*initialization of terminals*/
      :init_term->terminals
   QUEUES FOR QUEUEING TIME DIST:resp_time
      VALUES:.5 1 2 4 8
```

```
CONFIDENCE INTERVAL METHOD:spectral
INITIAL STATE DEFINITION-
CHAIN:c
   NODE LIST:init_term
   INIT POP: no_terms
CONFIDENCE LEVEL:90
SEQUENTIAL STOPPING RULE:yes
   CONFIDENCE INTERVAL QUEUES:resp_time resp_time
      MEASURES:                  qt         qtd
      ALLOWED WIDTHS:            10         10
INITIAL PORTION DISCARDED:10
INITIAL PERIOD LIMITS-
   QUEUES FOR DEPARTURE COUNTS:resp_time
      DEPARTURES:1000
LIMIT - CP SECONDS:100
TRACE:no
END
```

With these parameters, we expect very few collisions, if any, because it is unlikely that two or more stations would try to transmit at the same time. This is confirmed by the simulation:

```
RESQ2 VERSION DATE: JUNE 11, 1982 -  TIME: 12:02:07  DATE: 06/17/82
MODEL:CHAP6M2
ERROR: WARNING - NODE NOT BRANCHED TO: INIT_TERM
SAMPLING PERIOD END: RESP_TIME DEPARTURE LIMIT
SAMPLING PERIOD END: RESP_TIME DEPARTURE LIMIT
SAMPLING PERIOD END: RESP_TIME DEPARTURE LIMIT
SAMPLING PERIOD END: RESP_TIME DEPARTURE LIMIT
SAMPLING PERIOD END: RESP_TIME DEPARTURE LIMIT
SAMPLING PERIOD END: RESP_TIME DEPARTURE LIMIT
NO ERRORS DETECTED DURING SIMULATION.    609 DISCARDED EVENTS

                 SIMULATED TIME:     1.0720E+04
                      CPU TIME:          69.18
               NUMBER OF EVENTS:        40995
```

```
WHAT:nd
INVOCATION      ELEMENT         NUMBER OF DEPARTURES
                RESP_TIME       6832
                TERMINALSQ      10236
                NETWORKQ        3429
LAN             CABLE           13665
LAN             TIMING          27330
                END_RT          6832
                INIT_MSG        6833
                NET_REPLY       3429
                LOCAL_RPLY      3404
LAN             FINISHED        13665
LAN             ARRIVALS        13665
```

RESQ only reports the nodes with at least one departure during the run. Thus there were no collisions in this run.

```
WHAT:ut(lan.timing,lan.propagate,lan.capacity)
INVOCATION      ELEMENT        UTILIZATION
LAN             TIMING         1.0351E-03
LAN             PROPAGATE      4.2492E-06
LAN             CAPACITY       1.0308E-03


WHAT:qtbo(*)
INVOCATION      ELEMENT        MEAN QUEUEING TIME
                RESP_TIME      5.72917(5.52937,5.92897) 7.0%
                TERMINALSQ     9.96381
                NETWORKQ       1.48531
LAN             CABLE          8.1240E-04
LAN             TIMING         4.0599E-04
LAN             PROPAGATE      3.3333E-06
LAN             CAPACITY       8.0864E-04


WHAT:qtdbo
INVOCATION      ELEMENT        QUEUEING TIME DISTRIBUTION
                RESP_TIME      5.00E-01:0.16920(0.16004,0.17837) 1.8%
                               1.00E+00:0.29581(0.28790,0.30372) 1.6%
                               2.00E+00:0.46341(0.45202,0.47480) 2.3%
                               4.00E+00:0.63203(0.61769,0.64636) 2.9%
                               8.00E+00:0.77488(0.76389,0.78587) 2.2%

WHAT:
CONTINUE RUN:no
```

If we increase the number of terminals to 500, we do get a few collisions:

```
RESQ2 VERSION DATE: JUNE 11, 1982 -  TIME: 12:37:00  DATE: 06/17/82
MODEL:CHAP6M2H
ERROR: WARNING - NODE NOT BRANCHED TO: INIT_TERM
SAMPLING PERIOD END: RESP_TIME DEPARTURE LIMIT
SAMPLING PERIOD END: RESP_TIME DEPARTURE LIMIT
SAMPLING PERIOD END: RESP_TIME DEPARTURE LIMIT
SAMPLING PERIOD END: RESP_TIME DEPARTURE LIMIT
SAMPLING PERIOD END: RESP_TIME DEPARTURE LIMIT
RUN END: CPU LIMIT
NO ERRORS DETECTED DURING SIMULATION.   945 DISCARDED EVENTS

            SIMULATED TIME:     189.42805
                 CPU TIME:         100.78
            NUMBER OF EVENTS:       35824
```

```
WHAT:nd
INVOCATION         ELEMENT         NUMBER OF DEPARTURES
                   RESP_TIME       5931
                   TERMINALSQ      8966
                   NETWORKQ        2973
LAN                CABLE           11944
LAN                TIMING          23879
LAN                RETRYQ          6
                   END_RT          5931
                   INIT_MSG        6008
                   NET_REPLY       2973
                   LOCAL_RPLY      3036
LAN                COLLIDED        6
LAN                FINISHED        11938
LAN                COLLIDE         3
LAN                CLEAR           3
LAN                ARRIVALS        11945


WHAT:ut(lan.timing,lan.propagate,lan.capacity)
INVOCATION         ELEMENT         UTILIZATION
LAN                TIMING          0.05139
LAN                 PROPAGATE      2.1012E-04
LAN                 CAPACITY       0.05118
```

However, there is no significant effect on mean response time,

```
WHAT:qtbo(*)
INVOCATION         ELEMENT         MEAN QUEUEING TIME
                   RESP_TIME       5.53182(5.15682,5.90682) 13.6%
                   TERMINALSQ      9.48699
                   NETWORKQ        1.49810
LAN                CABLE           8.6210E-04
LAN                TIMING          4.0765E-04
LAN                 PROPAGATE      3.3333E-06
LAN                 CAPACITY       8.1206E-04
LAN                RETRYQ          1.2209E-03
```

and a maximum of two colliding stations:

```
WHAT:mxql(*)
INVOCATION         ELEMENT         MAXIMUM QUEUE LENGTH
                   RESP_TIME       209
                   TERMINALSQ      489
                   NETWORKQ        42
LAN                CABLE           4
LAN                TIMING          1
LAN                 PROPAGATE      1
LAN                 CAPACITY       1
LAN                RETRYQ          2
```

```
WHAT:
CONTINUE RUN:no
```

6.3. TOKEN PROTOCOLS

A primary competitor with CSMA/CD protocols for use in local networks is the token ring. (The word "token" is used in its common sense, to refer to a special control message, and has no other relationship to our use of "token" with respect to passive queues. We will be careful to avoid ambiguity as to which meaning of "token" we are using. The reader should also be careful.) A token ring may be viewed as a large shift register connecting the stations in a circle. A station wishing to transmit must wait until it receives the token message. The station may then transmit one data message on the ring and then retransmits the token message.

The data rate for a token ring is typically of the same order as a CSMA/CD network, 1-10 megabits per second. The token message is typically 8 bits. Simulation of the token ring is quite similar conceptually to the polling protocol simulation, but there is a qualitative difference. In simulating the polling protocol, the simulation of the polling when there was no traffic on the line was expensive but, perhaps, tolerable. In simulating a token ring with data message events on the order of seconds or milliseconds, it is totally impractical to simulate the movement of the token message around the idle ring, since that movement requires at most eight microseconds of simulated time and involves at least one simulated event per station.

Our extended queueing network representation of the token ring does not attempt to simulate the movement of the token message during periods when there is no data activity on the ring. Rather, when a data message is to be transmitted, a new token message is created and the data message waits for the newly created token message to have time to get around the ring. Our representation does not take into consideration the possibility that some other station might begin transmission before the station which created the new token message. The job representing the token message simply has a delay which is uniformly distributed between the minimum time needed for it to get to the station (zero) and the maximum time (the time to go all the way around the ring).

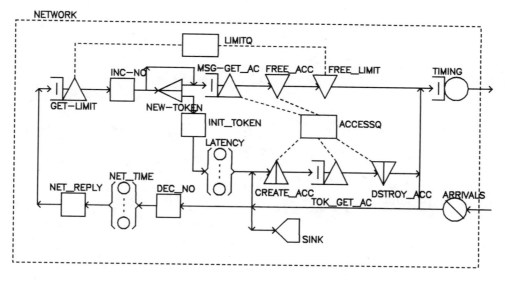

Figure 6.3 - Token Ring Bridge Representation

Unlike the previous two examples, where we could easily avoid explicit representation of individual stations, with the token ring we find it appropriate to explicitly represent the stations. Except for this difference, we use the same representations of the terminals and the bridge to the long haul network. Figure 6.3 shows the representation of the station bridging to the long haul network. In this figure the entire representation is of the token ring except for one set node and the network delay queue. Figure 6.4 is the corresponding figure for the terminal stations, which have additional detail beyond the token ring protocol. We do not show a figure for the connec-

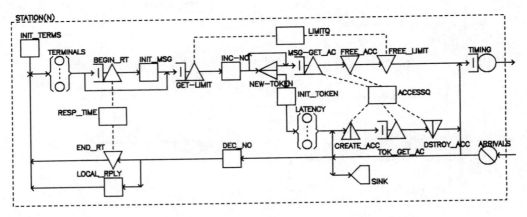

Figure 6.4 - Token Ring Terminal Representation

tion of the stations — the output of one station is connected to the input of its neighbor.

Passive queue "limitq" is used to limit a station to one transmission at a time. A message to be transmitted waits to allocate a token at "get__limit." Global variable "no__active" is used to count the number of active messages, i.e., messages ready for transmission, so that it can be determined whether it is necessary to generate a new token message. After a job gets the "limitq" token, it increments "no__active." It then goes to split node "new__token," if necessary, to generate a new token message.

Whether or not it generated a new token message, it then goes to allocate node "msg__get__ac" to wait for a passive queue token indicating it may transmit. When a token message reaches a station, it creates a token for passive queue "accessq" at node "create__acc." If there is a data message waiting (there can be at most one), it gets the "accessq" token and frees it at release node "free__acc." The data message frees the "limitq" token and goes to "timingq" for the delay in transmission to the neighbor. The token message gets the "accessq" token and destroys it at "destroy__acc." The token message goes to "timingq."

A data message arriving at its destination decrements "no__active" and then is handled as in the previous examples. A data message going through some other station goes directly to the next station after the timing delay. A token message arriving at a station after "no__active" has reached zero goes to the sink.

Following is the RESQ definition for the long haul network bridge submodel.

```
SUBMODEL:net_delay
   NUMERIC PARAMETERS:index
   CHAIN PARAMETERS:c
   QUEUE:limitq
      TYPE:passive
      TOKENS:1
      DSPL:fcfs
      ALLOCATE NODE LIST:get_limit
         NUMBERS OF TOKENS TO ALLOCATE:1
      RELEASE NODE LIST:free_limit
   QUEUE:accessq
      TYPE:passive
      TOKENS:0
      DSPL:fcfs
      ALLOCATE NODE LIST:msg_get_ac tok_get_ac
         NUMBERS OF TOKENS TO ALLOCATE:1
      RELEASE NODE LIST:free_acc
      DESTROY NODE LIST:dstroy_acc
      CREATE   NODE LIST:create_acc
         NUMBERS OF TOKENS TO CREATE:1
   QUEUE:timingq
      TYPE:fcfs
      CLASS LIST:timing
         SERVICE TIMES:standard(jv(msg_leng)/1.0E+06,0)
   QUEUE:latencyq
      TYPE:is
      CLASS LIST:latency
```

```
            SERVICE TIMES:uniform(0,1/3.0E+05,1)
    QUEUE:networkq
       TYPE:is
       CLASS LIST:net_time
           SERVICE TIMES:1.5
    SET NODES:net_reply
       ASSIGNMENT LIST:                                         ++
       jv(msg_leng)=standard(800,1)                             ++
       jv(msg_origin)=jv(terminal)                              ++
       jv(msg_dest)=jv(terminal)
    SET NODES:          inc_no              dec_no
       ASSIGNMENT LIST:no_active=no_active+1 no_active=no_active-1
    SET NODES:init_token
       ASSIGNMENT LIST:                                         ++
       jv(msg_type)=tok                                         ++
       jv(msg_leng)=8
    SPLIT NODES:new_token
    DUMMY NODES:arrivals
    CHAIN:c
       TYPE:external
       INPUT:arrivals
       OUTPUT:timing
       :arrivals->sink;if(/*jv(msg_type)=tok) and*/ no_active=0)
       :arrivals->create_acc;if(jv(msg_type)=tok)
       :arrivals->timing;if(jv(msg_dest)¬=index)
       :arrivals->dec_no->net_time->net_reply->get_limit
       :create_acc->tok_get_ac->dstroy_acc->timing
       :get_limit->inc_no->msg_get_ac new_token; ++
                       if(no_active>1) if(t)
       :msg_get_ac->free_acc->free_limit->timing
       :new_token->msg_get_ac init_token;split
       :init_token->latency->create_acc
END OF SUBMODEL NET_DELAY
```

This is the RESQ definition for the terminal station submodel:

```
SUBMODEL:station
    NUMERIC PARAMETERS:index
    CHAIN PARAMETERS:c
    QUEUE:terminalsq
       TYPE:is
       CLASS LIST:terminals
           SERVICE TIMES:thinktime
    QUEUE:resp_time /*response time*/
       TYPE:passive
       TOKENS:2147483647 /*"infinity"*/
       DSPL:fcfs
       ALLOCATE NODE LIST:begin_rt
           NUMBERS OF TOKENS TO ALLOCATE:1
       RELEASE NODE LIST: end_rt
    QUEUE:limitq
       TYPE:passive
```

```
      TOKENS:1
      DSPL:fcfs
      ALLOCATE NODE LIST:get_limit
          NUMBERS OF TOKENS TO ALLOCATE:1
      RELEASE NODE LIST:free_limit
  QUEUE:accessq
      TYPE:passive
      TOKENS:0
      DSPL:fcfs
      ALLOCATE NODE LIST:msg_get_ac tok_get_ac
          NUMBERS OF TOKENS TO ALLOCATE:1
      RELEASE NODE LIST:free_acc
      DESTROY NODE LIST:dstroy_acc
      CREATE   NODE LIST:create_acc
          NUMBERS OF TOKENS TO CREATE:1
  QUEUE:timingq
      TYPE:fcfs
      CLASS LIST:timing
          SERVICE TIMES:standard(jv(msg_leng)/1.0E+06,0)
  QUEUE:latencyq
      TYPE:is
      CLASS LIST:latency
          SERVICE TIMES:uniform(0,1/3.0E+05+8/1.0E+06,1)
                                /*propagation+capacity*/
  SET NODES:init_term
      ASSIGNMENT LIST:jv(terminal)=index
  SET NODES:init_msg
      ASSIGNMENT LIST:                                         ++
      jv(msg_type)=data                                        ++
      jv(msg_leng)=standard(800,1)                             ++
      jv(msg_origin)=jv(terminal)                              ++
      jv(msg_dest)=ceil(uniform(0,0,0.5;                       ++
       0,jv(terminal)-1,(jv(terminal)-1)/2*(no_terms-1);       ++
       jv(terminal),no_terms,(no_terms-jv(terminal))/2*(no_terms-1)))
  SET NODES:local_rply
      ASSIGNMENT LIST:                                         ++
      jv(msg_leng)=standard(800,1)                             ++
      jv(msg_origin)=jv(msg_dest)                              ++
      jv(msg_dest)=jv(terminal)
  SET NODES:          inc_no                    dec_no
      ASSIGNMENT LIST:no_active=no_active+1 no_active=no_active-1
  SET NODES:init_token
      ASSIGNMENT LIST:                                         ++
      jv(msg_type)=tok                                         ++
      jv(msg_leng)=8
  SPLIT NODES:new_token
  DUMMY NODES:arrivals
  CHAIN:c
      TYPE:external
      INPUT:arrivals
      OUTPUT:timing
      :arrivals->sink;if(/*jv(msg_type)=tok) and*/ no_active=0)
      :arrivals->create_acc;if(jv(msg_type)=tok)
```

```
        :arrivals->timing;if(jv(msg_dest)¬=index)
        :arrivals->dec_no->end_rt local_rply; ++
                        if(jv(msg_dest)=jv(terminal)) if(t)
        :create_acc->tok_get_ac->dstroy_acc->timing
        :end_rt local_rply->terminals
        :terminals->begin_rt get_limit; ++
                    if(th(resp_time)=0) if(t)
        :begin_rt->init_msg->get_limit
        :get_limit->inc_no->msg_get_ac new_token; ++
                        if(no_active>1) if(t)
        :msg_get_ac->free_acc->free_limit->timing
        :new_token->msg_get_ac init_token;split
        :init_token->latency->create_acc
      /*initialization of terminals*/
        :init_term->terminals
END OF SUBMODEL STATION
```

The model definition including these two submodels is as follows:

```
MODEL:chap6m3
    METHOD:simulation
    NUMERIC IDENTIFIERS:no_terms thinktime
        NO_TERMS:10
        THINKTIME:10
    NUMERIC IDENTIFIERS:msg_dest msg_leng msg_origin terminal msg_type
        MSG_DEST:0    /*JV to be used to indicate destination*/
        MSG_LENG:1    /*JV to be used to indicate length     */
        MSG_ORIGIN:2  /*JV to be used to indicate origin     */
        TERMINAL:3    /*JV to be used to indicate terminal   */
        MSG_TYPE:4    /*JV to be used to indicate type*/
    NUMERIC IDENTIFIERS:tok data
        TOK:1
        DATA:2
    GLOBAL VARIABLES:no_active
        NO_ACTIVE:0
    MAX JV:4
    INCLUDE:station
    INCLUDE:net_delay
```

An array of invocations is used for the terminal stations, with each element of the array given its index as a numeric parameter.

```
    INVOCATION:stations(no_terms)
        TYPE:station
        INDEX:(1 to no_terms by 1) /*list of 1,2,...,no_terms*/
        C:c
    INVOCATION:network
        TYPE:net_delay
        INDEX:0
        C:c
```

The "input" and "output" synonyms are left implicit in the following chain definition to simplify the iterative specification of connections between neighbors.

```
CHAIN:c
   TYPE:open
   :network->stations(1)
   :(for i=1 to no_terms-1 by 1):stations(i)->stations(i+1)
   :stations(10)->network
QUEUES FOR QUEUEING TIME DIST:stations(*).resp_time
   VALUES:.5 1 2 4 8
CONFIDENCE INTERVAL METHOD:spectral
INITIAL STATE DEFINITION-
CHAIN:c
   NODE LIST:stations(*).init_term
   INIT POP: 1
CONFIDENCE LEVEL:90
SEQUENTIAL STOPPING RULE:yes
   CONFIDENCE INTERVAL QUEUES:stations(1).resp_time
      MEASURES:              qt
      ALLOWED WIDTHS:        10
   CONFIDENCE INTERVAL QUEUES:stations(1).resp_time
      MEASURES:              qtd
      ALLOWED WIDTHS:        10
INITIAL PORTION DISCARDED:0
INITIAL PERIOD LIMITS-
   QUEUES FOR DEPARTURE COUNTS:stations(1).resp_time
      DEPARTURES:100
   LIMIT - CP SECONDS:2000
   TRACE:no
END
```

Since there are ten terminals, specifying a departure limit of 100 response times for one terminal is roughly equivalent to the previous specification of 1000 departures across all ten terminals. However, the specification of the stopping criteria is more stringent than before since the criteria are restricted to a single terminal. We get the following simulation results:

```
RESQ2 VERSION DATE: JUNE 18, 1982 -  TIME: 21:20:30  DATE: 06/17/82
MODEL:CHAP6M3
ERROR: WARNING - NODE NOT BRANCHED TO: STATIONS(1).INIT_TERM
ERROR: WARNING - NODE NOT BRANCHED TO: STATIONS(2).INIT_TERM
   ...
ERROR: WARNING - NODE NOT BRANCHED TO: STATIONS(10).INIT_TERM
SAMPLING PERIOD END: STATIONS(1).RESP_TIME DEPARTURE LIMIT
SAMPLING PERIOD END: STATIONS(1).RESP_TIME DEPARTURE LIMIT
SAMPLING PERIOD END: STATIONS(1).RESP_TIME DEPARTURE LIMIT
SAMPLING PERIOD END: STATIONS(1).RESP_TIME DEPARTURE LIMIT
SAMPLING PERIOD END: STATIONS(1).RESP_TIME DEPARTURE LIMIT
```

```
SAMPLING PERIOD END: STATIONS(1).RESP_TIME DEPARTURE LIMIT
SAMPLING PERIOD END: STATIONS(1).RESP_TIME DEPARTURE LIMIT
SAMPLING PERIOD END: STATIONS(1).RESP_TIME DEPARTURE LIMIT
SAMPLING PERIOD END: STATIONS(1).RESP_TIME DEPARTURE LIMIT
NO ERRORS DETECTED DURING SIMULATION.   3440 DISCARDED EVENTS

                    SIMULATED TIME:      3.6807E+04
                         CPU TIME:        1064.55
                 NUMBER OF EVENTS:         606377

WHAT:nd(stations(1),stations(*).resp_time)
INVOCATION       ELEMENT         NUMBER OF DEPARTURES
STATIONS(1)      RESP_TIME       2296
STATIONS(1)      LIMITQ          2448
STATIONS(1)      ACCESSQ         25758
STATIONS(1)        RELEASE       2448
STATIONS(1)        DESTROY       23310
STATIONS(1)      TERMINALSQ      2448
STATIONS(1)      TIMINGQ         46668
STATIONS(1)      LATENCYQ        2432
STATIONS(1)      RESP_TIME       2296
STATIONS(2)      RESP_TIME       2336
STATIONS(3)      RESP_TIME       2316
STATIONS(4)      RESP_TIME       2288
STATIONS(5)      RESP_TIME       2394
STATIONS(6)      RESP_TIME       2358
STATIONS(7)      RESP_TIME       2320
STATIONS(8)      RESP_TIME       2291
STATIONS(9)      RESP_TIME       2363
STATIONS(10)     RESP_TIME       2389

WHAT:qtbo(stations(*).resp_time)
INVOCATION       ELEMENT         MEAN QUEUEING TIME
STATIONS(1)      RESP_TIME       5.86521(5.59002,6.14040)  9.4%
STATIONS(2)      RESP_TIME       5.69031(5.29780,6.08282) 13.8%
STATIONS(3)      RESP_TIME       5.86568(5.48995,6.24141) 12.8%
STATIONS(4)      RESP_TIME       5.80673(5.44168,6.17178) 12.6%
STATIONS(5)      RESP_TIME       5.41839(5.17779,5.65898)  8.9%
STATIONS(6)      RESP_TIME       5.45440(5.13408,5.77473) 11.7%
STATIONS(7)      RESP_TIME       5.50468(5.24706,5.76230)  9.4%
STATIONS(8)      RESP_TIME       5.47117(5.31891,5.62342)  5.6%
STATIONS(9)      RESP_TIME       5.25881(4.95425,5.56336) 11.6%
STATIONS(10)     RESP_TIME       5.34525(4.98513,5.70536) 13.5%

WHAT:
CONTINUE RUN:no
```

CHAPTER 7

COMPUTER SYSTEM EXAMPLES

The examples of the last two chapters have dealt with communication issues and have largely ignored issues in the computers themselves. The purpose of this chapter is to illustrate how the same methodology applies to computer system modeling. We will focus on a three specific examples. These examples are extensions and variations on the examples associated with Figures 2.8 and 4.2. First we consider representation of multitasking, i.e., one activity being carried out by several cooperating processes. Then we consider spooling of peripheral devices. Finally, we develop a representation of interaction between disk devices and the channels (or controllers) which handle those devices.

7.1. MULTITASKING

The example of Figure 4.2 assumed that a user's command could be using the CPU or using a disk device, but not doing both at the same time. However, many operating systems will attempt to overlap CPU and I/O activity for a single job by allowing two or more tasks (processes) to perform work for that job. The tasks are synchronized at the occurrence of significant events, e.g., a computational task must wait for completion of an I/O task if its computations depend on data having been read or written by that task.

Figure 7.1 illustrates the modification of the network of Figure 4.2 to represent this overlapping of CPU-I/O activity for a single command. Our example will be optimistic about the degree of overlap. We assume that 50% of the CPU services are *potentially* overlapped with I/O, in the sense that overlap will occur if the jobs involved can both get the required servers. (In the system terminology, this would mean that the computational task would have the use of the processor at least part of the time that the I/O task would have the use of the device.) Even if the actual services are

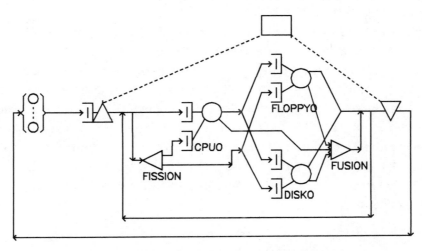

Figure 7.1 - CPU-I/O Multitasking

not overlapped, there may be some performance improvement because of overlap of times waiting for service.

In Figure 7.1 fission and fusion nodes are used to effect the potential overlap. With probability 0.5 a job receiving memory goes to the fission node instead of the CPU queue. The job which entered the fission node (the parent) then goes to a different class ("cpuo") than the jobs going to the CPU without going through the fission node. (The "o" suffix on the class names stands for "overlap.") One job is created at the fission node and goes to one of the disk queues, either to class "floppyo" or class "disko." Jobs leaving classes "cpuo", "floppyo" and "disko" go to the fusion node. When both a parent and its (sole) child are at the fusion node, the child disappears and the parent leaves the fusion node. The job leaving the fusion node may then go to the fission node again if it is to go back to the CPU.

From our discussion of fusion nodes, it should be clear that the classes "floppyo" and "disko" are not strictly necessary, i.e., the created jobs from the fission node could go to classes "floppy" and "disk" and all jobs leaving those classes could go to the fusion node. The fusion node would have no effect on the jobs that had not been through the fission node in the current CPU-I/O cycle.

Following is a RESQ dialogue file for this model.

```
MODEL:chap7m1
   METHOD:aplomb
   NUMERIC PARAMETERS:thinktime users pageframes
   NUMERIC IDENTIFIERS:floppytime disktime cputime
      FLOPPYTIME:.22
      DISKTIME:.019
      CPUTIME:.05
   NUMERIC IDENTIFIERS:cpiocycles
      CPIOCYCLES:8
   QUEUE:floppyq
      TYPE:fcfs
      CLASS LIST:floppy floppyo
         SERVICE TIMES:floppytime
   QUEUE:diskq
      TYPE:fcfs
      CLASS LIST:disk disko
         SERVICE TIMES:disktime
   QUEUE:cpuq
      TYPE:ps
      CLASS LIST:cpu cpuo
         SERVICE TIMES:cputime
   QUEUE:terminalsq
      TYPE:is
      CLASS LIST:terminals
         SERVICE TIMES:thinktime
   QUEUE:memory
      TYPE:passive
      TOKENS:pageframes
      DSPL:fcfs
      ALLOCATE NODE LIST:getmemory
         NUMBERS OF TOKENS TO ALLOCATE:discrete(16,.25;32,.5;48,.25)
      RELEASE NODE LIST:freememory
   FISSION NODES:fissionnod
   FUSION NODES:fusionnode
   CHAIN:interactiv
      TYPE:closed
      POPULATION:users
      :terminals->getmemory->fissionnod cpu;.5 .5
      :fissionnod->cpuo dummynode;fission
      :cpu->floppy disk;.1 .9
      :cpuo->fusionnode
      :dummynode->floppyo disko;.1 .9
      :floppyo disko->fusionnode
      :floppy->freememory cpu;1/cpiocycles (1-1/cpiocycles)*.5
      :floppy->fissionnod;(1-1/cpiocycles)*.5
```

```
      :disk->freememory cpu;1/cpiocycles (1-1/cpiocycles)*.5
      :disk->fissionnod;(1-1/cpiocycles)*.5
      :fusionnode->freememory cpu;1/cpiocycles (1-1/cpiocycles)*.5
      :fusionnode->fissionnod;(1-1/cpiocycles)*.5
      :freememory->terminals
  QUEUES FOR QUEUEING TIME DIST:memory
     VALUES:1 2 3 4 5 6 7 8
  CONFIDENCE INTERVAL METHOD:regenerative
  REGENERATION STATE DEFINITION-
  CHAIN:interactiv
     NODE LIST:terminals
     REGEN POP:users
     INIT POP:users
  CONFIDENCE LEVEL:90
  SEQUENTIAL STOPPING RULE:yes
     QUEUES TO BE CHECKED:memory
        MEASURES:qt
        ALLOWED WIDTHS:10
  SAMPLING PERIOD GUIDELINES-
     QUEUES FOR DEPARTURE COUNTS:memory
        DEPARTURES:2000
  LIMIT - CP SECONDS:300
  TRACE:no
END
```

We could get the following results, using the same parameters as before.

```
RESQ2 VERSION DATE: JUNE 11, 1982 -  TIME: 18:06:40  DATE: 06/17/82
MODEL:chap7m1
THINKTIME:10
USERS:30
PAGEFRAMES:128
SAMPLING PERIOD END: MEMORY DEPARTURE GUIDELINE
SAMPLING PERIOD END: MEMORY DEPARTURE GUIDELINE
SAMPLING PERIOD END: MEMORY DEPARTURE GUIDELINE
SAMPLING PERIOD END: MEMORY DEPARTURE GUIDELINE
SAMPLING PERIOD END: MEMORY DEPARTURE GUIDELINE
NO ERRORS DETECTED DURING SIMULATION.

                     SIMULATED TIME:    4453.97656
                          CPU TIME:      108.54
                 NUMBER OF EVENTS:       172316
                 NUMBER OF CYCLES:          313

WHAT:utbo
ELEMENT         UTILIZATION
MEMORY          0.82584(0.81276,0.83892) 2.6%
FLOPPYQ         0.40494(0.39290,0.41698) 2.4%
DISKQ           0.30932(0.30536,0.31329) 0.8%
CPUQ            0.90891(0.90048,0.91735) 1.7%
```

```
TERMINALSQ        0.00000(0.00000,0.00000)

WHAT:tpbo
ELEMENT           THROUGHPUT
MEMORY            2.28874(2.26657,2.31091) 1.9%
FLOPPYQ           1.83274(1.79455,1.87093) 4.2%
DISKQ             16.36693(16.18715,16.54672) 2.2%
CPUQ              18.19968(18.01088,18.38847) 2.1%
TERMINALSQ        2.28874(2.26657,2.31091) 1.9%
FREEMEMORY        2.28874
FISSIONNOD        9.08424
FUSIONNODE        9.08424
DUMMYNODE         9.08424

WHAT:qlbo
ELEMENT           MEAN QUEUE LENGTH
MEMORY            6.98981(6.67931,7.30030) 8.9%
FLOPPYQ           0.60410(0.57733,0.63088) 8.9%
DISKQ             0.41388(0.40671,0.42105) 3.5%
CPUQ              2.60553(2.55325,2.65781) 4.0%
TERMINALSQ        23.01019(22.69969,23.32068) 2.7%

WHAT:qtbo
ELEMENT           MEAN QUEUEING TIME
MEMORY            3.05400(2.90948,3.19851) 9.5%
FLOPPYQ           0.32962(0.32052,0.33871) 5.5%
DISKQ             0.02529(0.02501,0.02557) 2.2%
CPUQ              0.14316(0.14099,0.14534) 3.0%
TERMINALSQ        10.05365(9.90331,10.20399) 3.0%

WHAT:qtdbo
ELEMENT           QUEUEING TIME DISTRIBUTION
MEMORY            1.00E+00:0.19453(0.17485,0.21420) 3.9%
                  2.00E+00:0.38582(0.35846,0.41317) 5.5%
                  3.00E+00:0.56435(0.53643,0.59227) 5.6%
                  4.00E+00:0.70875(0.68376,0.73374) 5.0%
                  5.00E+00:0.82117(0.80119,0.84114) 4.0%
                  6.00E+00:0.89327(0.87877,0.90778) 2.9%
                  7.00E+00:0.93800(0.92657,0.94944) 2.3%
                  8.00E+00:0.96439(0.95616,0.97262) 1.6%

WHAT:
CONTINUE RUN:no
THINKTIME:
```

In Chapter 4 we did not give simulation results for the model without CPU-I/O overlap. The following is from the model without CPU-I/O overlap.

```
RESQ2 VERSION DATE: MARCH 11, 1982 - TIME: 20:53:25  DATE: 03/16/82
MODEL:chap7m2
THINKTIME:10
USERS:30
PAGEFRAMES:128
SAMPLING PERIOD END: MEMORY DEPARTURE GUIDELINE
SAMPLING PERIOD END: MEMORY DEPARTURE GUIDELINE
SAMPLING PERIOD END: MEMORY DEPARTURE GUIDELINE
SAMPLING PERIOD END: MEMORY DEPARTURE GUIDELINE
SAMPLING PERIOD END: MEMORY DEPARTURE GUIDELINE
SAMPLING PERIOD END: MEMORY DEPARTURE GUIDELINE
NO ERRORS DETECTED DURING SIMULATION.

                SIMULATED TIME:    5605.87500
                     CPU TIME:          95.89
             NUMBER OF EVENTS:         214365
             NUMBER OF CYCLES:            247


WHAT:qtbo(memory)
ELEMENT        MEAN QUEUEING TIME
MEMORY         3.40792(3.24079,3.57505) 9.8%


WHAT:
CONTINUE RUN:no
THINKTIME:
```

The multitasking seems to have produced a noticeable decrease in mean response time.

7.2. SPOOLING

The examples in this section and in Section 7.3 will be based on the central server model of Figure 2.8, i.e., we will not consider the terminals or memory explicitly. The computer system models we have looked at so far have (implicitly) considered use of disk devices for files and for paging but not for files spooled to or from slower devices such as printers. We now consider addition of printer spooling to the central server model.

Let us assume that there is a 300 line per minute printer supported by the computer system and that there are two tasks constantly present which handle the spooling. One task fills buffers from the disk for the printer and the other dumps the buffers to the printer. There are two buffers for the printer and each buffer contains 30 lines. Thus the transfer time for one buffer is 6 seconds (30/(300/60)).

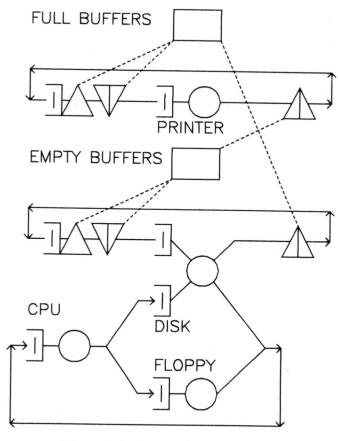

Figure 7.2 - Printer Spooling

Figure 7.2 shows the additions to the central server model. To represent the printer spooling we have two chains, one for each task, and two
passive queues, one for full buffers and one for empty buffers. The passive
queues will be used, in part, to represent communication between the tasks,
corresponding to the use of semaphores and similar task communication
primitives in operating systems. The number of tokens of each queue will
fluctuate between zero and two, because of create and destroy nodes, and
the total number of tokens will usually be less than two. The task which
empties the buffers acquires a token representing a full buffer, destroys it,
transfers the buffer contents to the printer and creates a token of the pool

representing empty buffers. Similarly, the task which fills the buffers acquires an "empty buffer" token, destroys it, transfers from the disk to the buffer and creates a token of the "full buffer" pool. The buffer emptying task waits at the full buffer allocate node when no full buffers are available, and the buffer filling task waits at the empty buffer allocate node when no empty buffers are available.

Following is a RESQ dialogue file for this model.

```
MODEL:chap7m3
   METHOD:simulation
   NUMERIC IDENTIFIERS:floppytime disktime cputime dmp
      FLOPPYTIME:.22
      DISKTIME:.019
      CPUTIME:.05
      DMP:4 /*Degree of multiprogramming*/
   NUMERIC IDENTIFIERS:buffers initfulbuf
      BUFFERS:2
      INITFULBUF:2
   NUMERIC IDENTIFIERS:lpm /*lines/minute*/ lpb /*lines/buffer*/
      LPM:300
      LPB:30
   QUEUE:floppyq
      TYPE:fcfs
      CLASS LIST:floppy
         SERVICE TIMES:floppytime
   QUEUE:diskq
      TYPE:fcfs
      CLASS LIST:disk diskspool
         SERVICE TIMES:disktime
   QUEUE:cpuq
      TYPE:ps
      CLASS LIST:cpu
         SERVICE TIMES:cputime
   QUEUE:printerq
      TYPE:fcfs
      CLASS LIST:printer
         SERVICE TIMES:standard(lpb/(lpm/60),0)
   QUEUE:fullbuffer
      TYPE:passive
      TOKENS:initfulbuf-1
      DSPL:fcfs
      ALLOCATE NODE LIST:getfullbuf
         NUMBERS OF TOKENS TO ALLOCATE:1
      DESTROY NODE LIST:destfulbuf
      CREATE NODE LIST:genfullbuf
         NUMBERS OF TOKENS TO CREATE:1
   QUEUE:empbuffer
      TYPE:passive
      TOKENS:buffers-initfulbuf
```

```
            DSPL:fcfs
            ALLOCATE NODE LIST:getempbuf
                NUMBERS OF TOKENS TO ALLOCATE:1
            DESTROY NODE LIST:destempbuf
            CREATE NODE LIST:genempbuf
                NUMBERS OF TOKENS TO CREATE:1
         CHAIN:csm
            TYPE:closed
            POPULATION:dmp
            :cpu->disk floppy;.9 .1
            :disk floppy->cpu
         CHAIN:emptying
            TYPE:closed
            POPULATION:1
            :getfullbuf->destfulbuf->printer->genempbuf->getfullbuf
         CHAIN:filling
            TYPE:closed
            POPULATION:1
            :getempbuf->destempbuf->diskspool->genfullbuf->getempbuf
         CONFIDENCE INTERVAL METHOD:regenerative
         REGENERATION STATE DEFINITION -
         CHAIN:csm
            NODE LIST:cpu
            REGEN POP:dmp
            INIT POP:dmp
         CHAIN:emptying
            NODE LIST:printer
            REGEN POP:1
            INIT POP:1
         CHAIN:filling
            NODE LIST:getempbuf
            REGEN POP:1
            INIT POP:1
         CONFIDENCE LEVEL:90
         SEQUENTIAL STOPPING RULE:yes
            QUEUES TO BE CHECKED:floppyq diskq printerq
                MEASURES:ut ut ut
                ALLOWED WIDTHS:10 10 10
         SAMPLING PERIOD GUIDELINES -
            QUEUES FOR DEPARTURE COUNTS:cpuq
                DEPARTURES:10000
         LIMIT - CP SECONDS:250
         TRACE:no
   END
```

We choose to use the **RESQ** regenerative method implementation in a heuristic manner, though we could use independent replications instead. (The spectral method would not provide confidence intervals for the performance measures we wish to examine.) Following are simulation results for the model.

RESQ2 VERSION DATE: MARCH 11, 1982 - TIME: 18:53:25 DATE: 03/16/82
MODEL: chap7m3
WARNING -- SOME PASSIVE QUEUE QT PROCESSES MAY
           NOT BE TRULY REGENERATIVE BECAUSE OF
           QUEUEING TIMES IN PROGRESS
WARNING -- MODEL MAY NOT BE TRULY REGENERATIVE
           BECAUSE OF NON-ZERO POPULATION AT CLASS
           WITH DIST. OTHER THAN BRANCHING ERLANG
SAMPLING PERIOD END: CPUQ DEPARTURE GUIDELINE
SAMPLING PERIOD END: CPUQ DEPARTURE GUIDELINE
NO ERRORS DETECTED DURING SIMULATION.

```
              SIMULATED TIME:      1055.25220
                    CPU TIME:         33.36
           NUMBER OF EVENTS:          40350
           NUMBER OF CYCLES:           8317
```

WHAT: utbo(*)
```
ELEMENT          UTILIZATION
FULLBUFFER       0.00000
EMPBUFFER        0.00000
FLOPPYQ          0.41176(0.36190,0.46162) 10.0%
DISKQ            0.32471(0.31889,0.33053) 1.2%
 DISK            0.32191(0.31611,0.32772) 1.2%
 DISKSPOOL       2.7956E-03(-5.6492E-04,6.1562E-03) 0.7%
CPUQ             0.95834(0.95279,0.96389) 1.1%
PRINTERQ         1.00000(0.99992,1.00008) 0.0%
```

WHAT: qlbo(*)
```
ELEMENT          MEAN QUEUE LENGTH
FULLBUFFER       0.00000
  DESTROY        0.00000
EMPBUFFER        0.99528(0.98976,1.00080) 1.1%
  DESTROY        0.99030
FLOPPYQ          0.63072(0.51490,0.74653) 36.7%
DISKQ            0.46227(0.44977,0.47476) 5.4%
 DISK            0.45754(0.44516,0.46993) 5.4%
 DISKSPOOL       4.7232E-03(-7.9525E-04,1.0242E-02) 233.7%
CPUQ             2.91174(2.86889,2.95459) 2.9%
PRINTERQ         1.00000(0.99992,1.00008) 0.0%
```

WHAT: tpbo(*)
```
ELEMENT          THROUGHPUT
FULLBUFFER       0.16584(0.03030,0.30138) 163.5%
EMPBUFFER        0.16584(0.03030,0.30138) 163.5%
FLOPPYQ          1.93792(1.77106,2.10479) 17.2%
DISKQ            17.18071(16.95303,17.40837) 2.7%
 DISK            17.01488(16.78821,17.24153) 2.7%
 DISKSPOOL       0.16584(0.03030,0.30138) 163.5%
CPUQ             18.95280(18.73048,19.17511) 2.3%
PRINTERQ         0.16584(0.03030,0.30138) 163.5%
```

```
WHAT:
CONTINUE RUN:no
```

With these parameters, the spooling has little impact on the rest of the system.

7.3. CHANNEL-DEVICE INTERACTION

The computer system models so far have assumed that competition between disks, e.g., for channels or controllers, is not significant. Let us consider a computer system with two disks where the same channel must be used to initiate positioning (arm and/or rotational) and for transfers. If the channel is not available when a device is in the correct rotational position, a job must wait a full revolution before it can try again to get the channel and make the transfer. Thus there may be substantial added delay if there is significant competition for the channel.

Figure 7.3 illustrates substantial additions to the central server model to represent channel contention and interactions between the channel and disk devices. This model also contains a submodel representation of round robin scheduling at the CPU. The I/O system is described as a submodel, with nested submodels for each disk. In the I/O system model there is a passive queue representing the channel, with node parameters to allow the nested submodels access to the channel passive queue. Within the disk submodel there is both a passive and an active queue representing the disk device. The passive queue is used for representing contention and the active queue is used for representing timing; there will never be more than one job at the (device) active queue.

After a job leaves the CPU and acquires the token for a device, it requests the channel, to initiate arm or rotational positioning. As soon as it gets the channel it releases it; we assume the time to initiate positioning is negligible, but that the time waiting to initiate positioning may not be negligible. The device arm may or may not be at the proper cylinder. We assume that with probability 2/3 the arm is already at the right cylinder and the job only needs to wait for rotational positioning. If the arm is not at the right cylinder we assume each of the remaining cylinders is equally likely to be the correct one. Global variables are used to keep track of the cur-

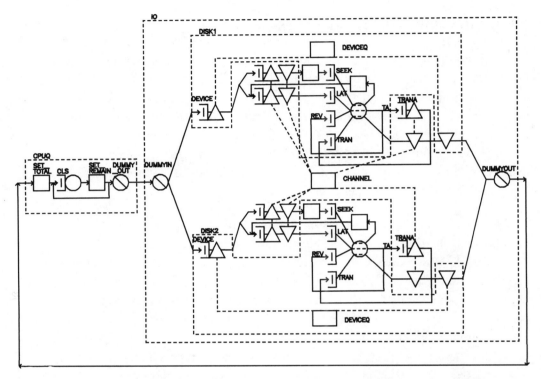

Figure 7.3 - Channel-Device Interaction

rent and chosen cylinder. After a seek the job initiates and waits for
rotational positioning. The rotational positioning time is uniformly distributed from 0 to one revolution.

After the device is at the correct rotational position, the TA (number
of tokens available) status function is used to determine whether the channel is available. If it is not, then the job is delayed for a full revolution.
Once the job gets the channel, it has a transfer time (which we assume to
be constant, e.g., one page) and then releases the channel and device. The
degree of multiprogramming is assumed constant.

Following is the dialogue file for the I/O subsystem submodel:

```
SUBMODEL:iosys /*subsystem with device contention for channel*/
   CHAIN PARAMETERS:c
   NUMERIC IDENTIFIERS:movearmp
      MOVEARMP:1/3
   QUEUE:channel
      TYPE:passive
      TOKENS:1
      DSPL:fcfs
      ALLOCATE NODE LIST:pos_s_a1 pos_l_a1 trana1
         NUMBERS OF TOKENS TO ALLOCATE:1
      ALLOCATE NODE LIST:pos_s_a2 pos_l_a2 trana2
         NUMBERS OF TOKENS TO ALLOCATE:1
      RELEASE NODE LIST:pos_s_r1 pos_l_r1 tranr1
      RELEASE NODE LIST:pos_s_r2 pos_l_r2 tranr2
   DUMMY NODES:dummyin dummyout
   SUBMODEL:dasd /*individual device*/
      NUMERIC PARAMETERS:ncyl startarmt cylt revt trant
      NODE PARAMETERS:pos_s_a pos_s_r pos_l_a pos_l_r trana tranr
      CHAIN PARAMETERS:c
      GLOBAL VARIABLE IDENTIFIERS:oldcyl newcyl
         OLDCYL:ncyl/2
         NEWCYL:0
      QUEUE:deviceq
         TYPE:passive
         TOKENS:1
         DSPL:fcfs
         ALLOCATE NODE LIST:device
            NUMBERS OF TOKENS TO ALLOCATE:1
         RELEASE NODE LIST:devicer
      QUEUE:timesq
         TYPE:fcfs
         CLASS LIST:seek
            SERVICE TIMES:standard(startarmt+abs(newcyl-oldcyl) ++
                                               *cylt,0)
         CLASS LIST:lat rev
            SERVICE TIMES:uniform(0,revt,1) standard(revt,0)
         CLASS LIST:tran
            SERVICE TIMES:standard(trant,0)
      SET NODES:setnewcyl
      ASSIGNMENT LIST:++
         newcyl=ceil(uniform(0,oldcyl-1,(oldcyl-1)/(ncyl-1);++
                        oldcyl,ncyl,(ncyl-oldcyl)/(ncyl-1)))
      SET NODES:setoldcyl
      ASSIGNMENT LIST:oldcyl=newcyl
      CHAIN:c
         TYPE:external
         INPUT:device
         OUTPUT:devicer
         :device->pos_s_a pos_l_a;movearmp 1-movearmp
         :pos_s_a->pos_s_r->setnewcyl->seek->setoldcyl->pos_l_a
```

```
            :pos_l_a->pos_l_r->lat
            :lat->trana rev;if(ta>0) if(t)
            :rev->trana rev;if(ta>0) if(t)
            :trana->tran->tranr->devicer
      END OF SUBMODEL DASD
      INVOCATION:disk1
         TYPE:dasd
         NCYL:800
         STARTARMT:.01
         CYLT:.0001
         REVT:.0166667
         TRANT:.0029
         POS_S_A:pos_s_a1
         POS_S_R:pos_s_r1
         POS_L_A:pos_l_a1
         POS_L_R:pos_l_r1
         TRANA:trana1
         TRANR:tranr1
         C:c
      INVOCATION:disk2
         TYPE:dasd
         NCYL:800
         STARTARMT:.01
         CYLT:.0001
         REVT:.0166667
         TRANT:.0029
         POS_S_A:pos_s_a2
         POS_S_R:pos_s_r2
         POS_L_A:pos_l_a2
         POS_L_R:pos_l_r2
         TRANA:trana2
         TRANR:tranr2
         C:c
      CHAIN:c
         TYPE:external
         INPUT:dummyin
         OUTPUT:dummyout
         :dummyin->disk1.input disk2.input;.5 .5
         :disk1.output disk2.output->dummyout
END OF SUBMODEL IOSYS
```

The submodel representing round robin scheduling uses a job variable to store the total service time for a given visit to the CPU. The queue itself has FCFS scheduling, with the service time based on the minimum of the remaining service and the round robin quantum.

```
SUBMODEL:rrqueue /*round robin queue*/
   NUMERIC PARAMETERS:mean_serve quantum overhead
   CHAIN PARAMETERS:chn
   QUEUE:q
      TYPE:fcfs
```

```
        CLASS LIST:cls
            SERVICE TIMES:standard(min(jv(0),quantum)+overhead,0)
    SET NODES:set_total
    ASSIGNMENT LIST:jv(0)=standard(mean_serve,1)
    SET NODES:set_remain
    ASSIGNMENT LIST:jv(0)=jv(0)-min(jv(0),quantum)
    DUMMY NODES:dummy_out
    CHAIN:chn
        TYPE:external
        INPUT:set_total
        OUTPUT:dummy_out
        :set_total->cls->set_remain->cls dummy_out;if(jv(0)>0) if(t)
    END OF SUBMODEL RRQUEUE
```

Following is the model definition invoking these submodels.

```
MODEL:chap7m4
    METHOD:simulation
    NUMERIC IDENTIFIERS:mean_serve quantum overhead
        MEAN_SERVE:.02
        QUANTUM:.02
        OVERHEAD:.0002
    INCLUDE:rrqueue
    INCLUDE:iosys
    INVOCATION:cpuq
        TYPE:rrqueue: mean_serve; quantum; overhead; c
    INVOCATION:io
        TYPE:iosys
        C:c
    CHAIN:c
        TYPE:closed
        POPULATION:4
        :cpuq.output->io.input
        :io.output->cpuq.input
    CONFIDENCE INTERVAL METHOD:replications
    INITIAL STATE DEFINITION -
    CHAIN:c
        NODE LIST:cpuq.set_total
        INIT POP:4
    CONFIDENCE LEVEL:90
    NUMBER OF REPLICATIONS:5
    INITIAL PORTION DISCARDED:10 /*percent*/
    REPLIC LIMITS-
        NODES FOR DEPARTURE COUNTS:cpuq.set_total
            DEPARTURES:10000
    LIMIT - CP SECONDS:300
    TRACE:no
END
```

Following are the simulation results.

```
RESQ2 VERSION DATE: MARCH 3, 1982 -  TIME: 22:29:10  DATE: 03/09/82
MODEL:chap7m4
REPLICATION   1: SET_TOTAL DEPARTURE LIMIT
REPLICATION   2: SET_TOTAL DEPARTURE LIMIT
REPLICATION   3: SET_TOTAL DEPARTURE LIMIT
REPLICATION   4: SET_TOTAL DEPARTURE LIMIT
REPLICATION   5: SET_TOTAL DEPARTURE LIMIT
NO ERRORS DETECTED DURING SIMULATION.  19837 DISCARDED EVENTS

     SIMULATED TIME PER REPLICATION:      207.52304
                        CPU TIME:          291.46
  NUMBER OF EVENTS PER REPLICATION:        35782
          NUMBER OF REPLICATIONS:             5


WHAT:tpbo
INVOCATION INVOCATION ELEMENT      THROUGHPUT
           CPUQ       Q            68.54985(68.37177,68.72792) 0.5%
           IO         CHANNEL      101.30110(100.28430,102.31792) 2.0%
IO         DISK1      DEVICEQ      21.86382(21.54640,22.18124) 2.9%
IO         DISK1      TIMESQ       52.40106(51.56384,53.23827) 3.2%
IO         DISK2      DEVICEQ      21.50816(21.28053,21.73578) 2.1%
IO         DISK2      TIMESQ       51.48280(50.97803,51.98758) 2.0%
           CPUQ       SET_TOTAL    43.36867
           CPUQ       SET_REMAIN   68.54947
           CPUQ       DUMMY_OUT    43.37251
           IO         POS_S_R1     7.35436
           IO         POS_L_R1     21.86263
           IO         TRANR1       21.86166
           IO         POS_S_R2     7.20016
           IO         POS_L_R2     21.50700
           IO         TRANR2       21.50700
           IO         DUMMYIN      43.37251
           IO         DUMMYOUT     43.36867
IO         DISK1      DEVICER      21.86166
IO         DISK1      SETNEWCYL    7.35436
IO         DISK1      SETOLDCYL    7.35340
IO         DISK2      DEVICER      21.50700
IO         DISK2      SETNEWCYL    7.20016
IO         DISK2      SETOLDCYL    7.20016


WHAT:utbo(cpuq.q,io.channel,io.disk1.deviceq,io.disk2.deviceq)
INVOCATION INVOCATION ELEMENT      UTILIZATION
           CPUQ       Q            0.87926(0.87447,0.88406) 1.0%
           IO         CHANNEL      0.12578(0.12460,0.12696) 0.2%
IO         DISK1      DEVICEQ      0.53930(0.52858,0.55002) 2.1%
IO         DISK2      DEVICEQ      0.52685(0.52173,0.53196) 1.0%


WHAT:qlbo(*)
INVOCATION INVOCATION ELEMENT      MEAN QUEUE LENGTH
           CPUQ       Q            2.21399(2.18089,2.24708) 3.0%
           IO         CHANNEL      0.12935(0.12820,0.13050) 1.8%
           IO         POS_S_A1     3.65E-04(2.95E-04,4.34E-04) 38.0%
           IO         POS_L_A1     1.39E-03(1.30E-03,1.48E-03) 13.1%
```

	IO	TRANA1	0.06341(0.06248,0.06433) 2.9%
	IO	POS_S_A2	4.02E-04(3.75E-04,4.29E-04) 13.3%
	IO	POS_L_A2	1.42E-03(1.32E-03,1.51E-03) 13.3%
	IO	TRANA2	0.06237(0.06171,0.06303) 2.1%
IO	DISK1	DEVICEQ	0.91284(0.87976,0.94592) 7.2%
IO	DISK1	TIMESQ	0.53754(0.52681,0.54828) 4.0%
IO	DISK1	SEEK	0.27007(0.26338,0.27675) 5.0%
IO	DISK1	LAT	0.18209(0.17829,0.18589) 4.2%
IO	DISK1	REV	0.02198(0.02002,0.02394) 17.8%
IO	DISK1	TRAN	0.06341(0.06248,0.06433) 2.9%
IO	DISK2	DEVICEQ	0.87317(0.86327,0.88307) 2.3%
IO	DISK2	TIMESQ	0.52503(0.51989,0.53017) 2.0%
IO	DISK2	SEEK	0.26165(0.25638,0.26693) 4.0%
IO	DISK2	LAT	0.17991(0.17757,0.18225) 2.6%
IO	DISK2	REV	0.02109(0.02007,0.02212) 9.7%
IO	DISK2	TRAN	0.06237(0.06171,0.06303) 2.1%

WHAT:st(*)

INVOCATION	INVOCATION	ELEMENT	MEAN SERVICE TIMES
	CPUQ	Q	0.01283
IO	DISK1	TIMESQ	0.01026
IO	DISK1	SEEK	0.03671
IO	DISK1	LAT	8.3271E-03
IO	DISK1	REV	0.01667
IO	DISK1	TRAN	2.9000E-03
IO	DISK2	TIMESQ	0.01020
IO	DISK2	SEEK	0.03634
IO	DISK2	LAT	8.3646E-03
IO	DISK2	REV	0.01667
IO	DISK2	TRAN	2.9000E-03

WHAT:gv

INVOCATION	INVOCATION	ELEMENT	FINAL VALUES OF GLOBAL VARIABLES
	IO	DISK1	OLDCYL	119.00000
IO	DISK1	NEWCYL	119.00000
IO	DISK2	OLDCYL	645.00000
IO	DISK2	NEWCYL	645.00000

WHAT:

CHAPTER 8

CONCLUSION

Computer communication systems are prevalent today. Many computer systems are connected together with high speed communication links and large numbers of terminals are connected to these computers, with lower speed links. These systems will continue to proliferate and systems based on local area networks will also become widespread. Performance modeling of these systems can be extremely valuable for their design, development and efficient operation. Computer communication systems are complex. In order to simplify the task of understanding how these systems perform, models should be used. Models can aid in predicting the behavior of systems which do not exist and in determining the effects of changes which are made to existing networks.

We discussed two types of modeling techniques. Analytic models consist of equations which relate parameters of the model to the performance measures. An analytic solution gives the exact results for the model which is being solved. A model which is solved using simulation can usually be formulated as a more exact representation of the real system than a corresponding analytic model. Simulation is a statistical experiment which imitates the behavior of the model and observes it as the state of the model changes. Since simulation produces random results, we use confidence intervals to determine the accuracy of the results.

We have appproached modeling in the context of queueing network models. The primary advantage of using a queueing network representation for simulation of computer communication systems is the high level of description used, in comparison with the conventional simulation programming languages. In using simulation, we can describe a system as a queueing network and incorporate any level of detail. Extended queueing networks provide additional network elements and powerful modeling constructs for the representation of complex situations found in real systems.

The basic problems in using queueing network models are to (1) determine which resources are important to have in the model and the characteristics which will most affect performance, (2) formulate a model representing these resources and characteristics, and (3) determine the values for the performance measures of the model. Item (1) requires that the modeler understand the system, and that he or she uses intuition in determining what is important. A model is a simplistic representation of the system. It is necessary to decide on how much detail the model will contain. In doing this, we must make many simplifying assumptions. The second problem involves a description of the flow of messages through the network and the amount of service required at the resources. For queueing network models to be used effectively for the representation of computer communication systems, appropriate software is needed. The Research Queueing Package provides many of the desireable properties of software for these types of models. Many of the examples discussed throughout the text have been illustrated with RESQ models. The ease with which complex situations can be represented has been demonstrated with these models.

Models should be developed in a top-down, hierarchical fashion. A model can never exactly represent the real system. The model should include only as much detail as is necessary to accurately produce the desired performance measures. Modeling should begin simply, with additional complexity being added as the system and the model are better understood. RESQ provides a facility for defining submodels which can be nested within each other. These submodels help give the model structure and allow for the addition of further details as they are necessary.

We have presented many different models of computer communication systems. Some of the models have dealt with protocols like acknowledgements, time-outs, packetizing of messages, adaptive routing and flow control. Models of local area networks have illustrated polled multidrop lines, CSMA/CD networks and token rings. Computer system models displayed examples of multitasking, spooling and channel-device interaction. The modeling techniques used in these models are applicable to current computer communication systems.

Systems are becoming increasingly complex. We need mathematical tools to help us understand the behavior of these systems. We have attempted to show how some of these complexities can be represented and studied. In the future, we will need tools which are simpler to use and which can represent even more complex conditions. We hope the ideas we have presented will aid in future modeling endeavors.

BIBLIOGRAPHY

1. C.E. Agnew, "On Quadratic Adaptive Routing Algorithms," *CACM 19*, 1 (January 1976) pp. 18-22.

2. F. Baskett, K.M. Chandy, R.R. Muntz and F.G. Palacios, "Open, Closed, and Mixed Networks of Queues with Different Classes of Customers," *JACM 22*, 2 (April 1975) pp. 248-260.

3. J.P. Buzen, *Queueing Network Models of Multiprogramming*, Ph.D. Thesis, Harvard University, Cambridge, Mass. (1971). Garland Publishing, New York (1980).

4. K.M. Chandy, J. Misra, R. Berry and D. Neuse, "Simulation Tools in Performance Evaluation," *CPEUG 81*, (Computer Performance Evaluation Users Group), San Antonio, Texas (November 1981).

5. P. Heidelberger and P.D. Welch, "A Spectral Method for Confidence Interval Generation and Run Length Control in Simulations," *CACM 24*, 4 (April 1981) pp. 233-245.

6. J. R. Jackson, "Jobshop-Like Queueing Systems," *Management Science 10*, 1 (October 1963) pp. 131-142.

7. L. Kleinrock, *Communication Nets: Stochastic Message Flow and Delay*, McGraw-Hill, New York (1964). Reprinted, Dover Publications (1972).

8. L. Kleinrock, *Queueing Systems Volume I: Theory*, Wiley, New York (1975).

9. L. Kleinrock, *Queueing Systems Volume II: Computer Applications*, Wiley, New York (1976).

10. A.G. Konheim and B. Meister, "Service in a Loop System," *JACM 19*, (January 1972) pp. 92-108.

11. S.S. Lam and Y.L. Lien, "A Tree Convolution Algorithm for the Solution of Queueing Networks," to appear, *CACM*.

12. S. S. Lavenberg and C. H. Sauer, "Analytical Results for Queueing Models," Chapter 3 of S. S. Lavenberg, editor, *Computer Performance Modeling Handbook,* Academic Press, Inc., New York (1983).

13. D. Merle, D. Potier and M. Veran, "A Tool for Computer System Performance Analysis," *Performance of Computer Installations,* Ferrari, D. (editor), North-Holland (1978).

14. M. Reiser and S.S. Lavenberg, "Mean Value Analysis of Closed Multichain Queueing Networks," *JACM 27,* 2 (April 1980) pp. 313-322.

15. M. Reiser and C.H. Sauer, "Queueing Network Models: Methods of Solution and their Program Implementation," in K.M. Chandy and R.T. Yeh, editors, *Current Trends in Programming Methodology, Volume III: Software Modeling and Its Impact on Performance.* Prentice-Hall (1978) pp. 115-167.

16. M. Reiser, "Performance Evaluation of Data Communication Systems," IBM Research Report RZ-1092 (August 1981).

17. C.H. Sauer, "Passive Queue Models of Computer Networks," *Computer Networking Symposium,* Gaithersburg, Maryland (December 1978). IEEE Catalog No. 78CH1400-1.

18. C.H. Sauer, "Computational Algorithms for State-Dependent Queueing Networks," *ACM Transactions on Computer Systems 1,* 1 (February 1983).

19. C.H. Sauer and K.M. Chandy, *Computer Systems Performance Modeling,* Prentice-Hall, Englewood Cliffs, NJ (1981).

20. C.H. Sauer and E.A. MacNair, "Queueing Network Software for Systems Modeling," *Software-Practice and Experience 9,* 5 (May 1979).

21. C. H. Sauer and E.A. MacNair, "Extended Queueing Network Models," Chapter 8 of S. S. Lavenberg, editor, *Computer Performance Modeling Handbook,* Academic Press, Inc., New York (1982).

22. C. H. Sauer and E.A. MacNair, "The Research Queueing Package Version 2: Availability Notice," IBM Research Report RA-144, Yorktown Heights, New York (August 1982).

23. C.H. Sauer, E.A. MacNair and J.F. Kurose, "The Research Queueing Package: Past, Present and Future," *Proceedings 1982 National Computer Conference.*

24. C.H. Sauer, E.A. MacNair and J.F. Kurose, "The Research Queueing Package Version 2: Introduction and Examples," IBM Research Report RA-138, Yorktown Heights, New York (April 1982).

25. C.H. Sauer, E.A. MacNair and J.F. Kurose, "The Research Queueing Package Version 2: CMS Users Guide," IBM Research Report RA-139, Yorktown Heights, New York (April 1982).

26. C.H. Sauer, E.A. MacNair and J.F. Kurose, "The Research Queueing Package Version 2: TSO Users Guide," IBM Research Report RA-140, Yorktown Heights, New York (April 1982).

27. C.H. Sauer, E.A. MacNair and S. Salza, "A Language for Extended Queueing Networks," *IBM J. of Research and Development 24,* 6 (November 1980).

28. C.H. Sauer, M. Reiser and E.A. MacNair, "RESQ - A Package for Solution of Generalized Queueing Networks," *Proceedings 1977 National Computer Conference.*

29. M. Schwartz, *Computer-Communication Network Design and Analysis,* Prentice-Hall (1977).

30. C.E. Skinner, "A Priority Queueing System with Server Walking Time," *Operations Research 15,* (1967) pp. 278-285.

31. A.S. Tanenbaum, *Computer Networks,* Prentice-Hall (1981).

32. A.S. Tanenbaum, "Network Protocols," *Computing Surveys 13,* 4 (December 1981) pp. 453-489.

33. S. Tucci and C.H. Sauer, "The Tree MVA Algorithm," IBM Research Report RC-9338 (April 1982).

34. P.D. Welch, "The Statistical Analysis of Simulation Results," S.S. Lavenberg (Editor), *Computer Performance Modeling Handbook,* to appear, Academic Press (1982).

INDEX

A

Absolute width   66
Acknowledgements   27, 50, 50, 81
   negative   91
Active queues   34, 35
Allocate nodes   48
Analytic models   4, 6
Array of invocations   128
Arrival processes   10
Arrival rates   41
Arrival times   36
Assignment statements   38, 42
Automated run length   58
Automated stopping rule   73

B

Boolean funtions   47
Buffer contention   91
Buffering   22
Bulk arrival mechanisms   50

C

Central server model   22, 136
Chain parameters   70
Chain variables   36, 38, 38, 40, 42,
   49
Chains   25, 36
   closed   37
   open   37
Children   51
Classes   14, 34, 35

Clock   43
Closed networks   22, 25
Coefficient of variation   44, 45, 45
Collisions   115
Confidence interval method   62
Confidence intervals   40, 55, 58,
   64, 66, 73
Confidence level   40, 55
Control messages   50
Correlations   57
Create nodes   50
CSMA/CD   114
CV   40

D

Data types   38
Destroy nodes   50
Diagrams   33
Dialogue files   59, 59
Discarded initial portions   57
Distribution functions   38
Distributions   43
   empirical   44
   Branching Erlang   44, 57
   BE   44, 44
   DISCRETE   44
   Erlang   44
   Exponential   45
   Hyperexponential   44, 45
   Hypoexponential   44, 45
   Performance measures   62
   STANDARD   44, 46
   UNIFORM   45, 113

Dummy nodes 76

E

Elements 33, 34, 36
Equilibrium behavior 56, 58
Ethernet 115
Events 63
Extended queueing networks 6, 8, 9, 33
External 72

F

Family 51
Fission nodes 39, 51, 85, 132
  nested 52
Fixed service rates 34
Flow controls 22, 25
Functions 37
Fusion nodes 50, 51, 51, 85, 132

G

Global variables 38, 38, 42, 49, 60, 96

H

Hierarchical definitions 69
Holding buffers 33

I

Independence assumption 18, 39, 67
Independent and identically distributed 56, 57
Independent replications 56
Infinite server 27, 35
Initial state 56, 62
Initialization 55
Input 72
Interarrival times 36, 41
Invocations 72
Invoking models 70
ISO OSI 7

J

Job variables 34, 37, 38, 39, 42, 49, 50, 60, 61
Jobs 10, 34, 35, 36
JV 39

L

Libraries 72
Line controllers 108
Link capacities 11
Local networks 1, 2, 8, 108
Long haul networks 1, 2, 108
Lost messages 84

M

M/G/1 queues 12
M/M/1 queues 10
Macro definitions 69
Mean queue lengths 11, 12, 19

Mean queueing times   12, 19, 58, 67

Mean response times   12, 19, 73

Mean service rates   10

Mean service times   10, 14, 15, 19, 23, 25

Mean Value Analysis   27

Memory contention   24

Memoryless property   57

Message classes   14

Messages   10

Method of exponential stages   44

Mixed networks   31

Model results

    chap4m1   63

    chap5m1   83, 95

    chap5m2   89

    chap5m3   100

    chap5m4   105

    chap6m1   113

    chap6m2   119

    chap6m2h   120

    chap6m3   129

    chap7m1   134

    chap7m2   135

    chap7m3   139

    chap7m4   145

Modeling   3

Models

    chap4m1   60

    chap5m1   79

    chap6m1   111

    chap6m2   117

    chap6m3   128

    chap7m1   133

    chap7m3   138

    chap7m4   145

csm   72

Modular representation   75

Multiple classes   25

Multiserver queues   31

Multitasking   131

N

Network definition   58

Networks of queues   4

Node parameters   72, 77

Nodes   36

Normalizing constant   27

O

Open networks   19

Output   72

Overlap   131

P

Packetizing   22, 33

Packets   51, 52, 92

Parallel activities   51

Parallelism   33

Parent   51

Passive queues   6, 33, 48, 52, 60, 61, 77

Performance evaluation   2, 3

Performance measures   4, 6, 23, 54, 55, 64

Point estimates   40, 55

Polling   108

Pool of tokens   48

Population (closed chain)   37

Predicates 47

Preemption 35

Priorities 16, 34, 110

   non-preemptive 79, 83

Probability distributions 35, 36,

   43, 49

Processor sharing 17, 23

Product form solution 4, 18, 22,

   27, 34, 47

Propagation delays 11

Protocols 22, 33, 50, 50

Q

Queue lengths 49

Queueing models 3, 33

Queueing network models 4, 9, 18

Queueing networks 4, 6, 18, 33

   extensions 6

Queueing time distributions 13, 58

Queueing times 48

R

Random number streams 55

Reassembly of messages 22, 33

Regeneration cycles 57, 63

Regeneration state 57, 63, 73

Regenerative method 57, 63, 73

Regenerative systems 57

Related jobs 51

Relative throughputs 28

Relative width 58, 64, 73

Relatives 51

Release nodes 49

Release of tokens 50, 61

Replication length 57

Resource sharing 3

Response times 33, 48

Routing 36

Routing chains 27

Routing definition 62

S

Semaphores 137

Sequential procedure 58

Servers 34, 35

Service capacities 31

Service processes 9, 10

Service rates 35

Service requirements 34

Service times 35

Set nodes 38, 60, 61

Simulation 4, 18, 33

Simulation run lengths 54, 55, 58

Simulation times 43

Simultaneous resource possession

   4, 33, 48

Single queue models 4, 9

Sink 34, 36, 37, 50

Sources 34, 35, 37, 62

Spectral Method 57

Split nodes 6, 37, 39, 50

Spooling 136

Standard deviations 12, 14, 15, 43

States 33, 47, 57

Statistical analysis 5, 7, 54, 74

Statistical variability 55

Status functions 38, 48, 85

Stopping criteria 58, 62

Store and forward buffering 91

Subchains 37

Submodels   70, 75
    city   78, 82, 86, 94, 98, 103
    csma__cd   115
    cssm   71
    dasd   143
    iosys   142
    net__delay   125
    poll__line   109
    rrqueue   144
    station   126
Symbols   35, 36, 48
Synchronization   33, 51
SNA   7

T

Throughput   10
Time outs   84
Token rings   122
Tokens   48

Transfer nodes   50, 52, 85
Transient behavior   56
Transmission times   11
True values   55

U

Utilization   10, 66

V

Variables   37

W

Waiting lines   35
Windows   25
Work demands   34, 35